WADSWORTH P

ON

SEARLE

William Hirstein
Elmhurst College

Australia • Canada • Mexico • Singapore • Spain
United Kingdom • United States

For Robert and Nancy

COPYRIGHT © 2001 Wadsworth, a division of Thomson Learning, Inc. Thomson Learning™ is a trademark used herein under license.

ALL RIGHTS RESERVED. No part of this work covered by the copyright hereon may be reproduced or used in any form or by any means—graphic, electronic, or mechanical, including photocopying, recording, taping, Web distribution, or information storage and retrieval systems—without the written permission of the publisher.

Printed in the United States of America
1 2 3 4 5 6 7 04 03 02 01 00

For permission to use material from this text, contact us:
Web: http://www.thomsonrights.com
Fax: 1-800-730-2215
Phone: 1-800-730-2214

For more information, contact:
Wadsworth/Thomson Learning, Inc.
10 Davis Drive
Belmont, CA 94002-3098
USA
http://www.wadsworth.com

ISBN: 0-534-57626-5

Contents

1. Intentionality — 1
Introduction — 1
Searle's Milieu — 2
Biological Naturalism — 5
Intentional States — 8

2. Language — 17
Introduction — 17
Speech Acts — 18
*The Description Theory of Reference vs.
    The Causal Theory* — 20
Against Quinean Indeterminacy — 26
Questions — 29

3. Mind — 34
Introduction — 35
The Chinese Room — 33
Consciousness as a Biological Phenomenon — 45
The Ontology and Epistemology of the Mental — 47
Introspection is Not Like Perception — 49
Relational vs. Intrinsic Theories of Awareness — 49
A Solution to The Mind-Body Problem — 55
*The Connection Between Consciousness
    and Intentionality* — 56
Intentionality and Intrinsicality — 59

4. Reality — 63
Introduction — 63
The Defense of Realism — 65
Searle's Ontology — 73
Truth as Correspondence — 73
Searle's Legacy — 74

Biographical Note — 79

Bibliography — 81
Selected Works — 81

Acknowledgements

I would like to thank Dan Primozic, Joel Thompson, Dan Kolak, and Joseph Sathiaraj for comments and suggestions. Special thanks to Melinda Campbell for our many discussions on Searle's philosophy over the years. Discussions with Thomas Natsoulas, V.S. Ramachandran, and Patricia Churchland have also been important in forming some of the criticisms I make here. Thanks also to John Searle for offering comments on parts of the book and for supplying biographical material.

1
Intentionality

Intrinsic intentionality is a phenomenon that humans and certain other animals have as part of their biological nature.

The Rediscovery of the Mind, 1992

Introduction

The core concept of Searle's philosophy is *intentionality*. Intentionality is a property of certain mental states which makes them about, or directed at, or represent, events in the world. Human beings are essentially representers of the world, and representation is the primary function of our minds. When we think, plan, conceive, or engage in a host of other mental acts, we are representing the world, and this makes our mental states *intentional states*, in Searle's terminology. Words also represent, or refer, but only because of the representational capacities contained in the minds of language users. The intentionality which printed or spoken words possess is in Searle's terminology *derived* intentionality, as opposed to the *intrinsic* intentionality possessed only by intentional states.

A second important concept in Searle's work is consciousness. It is his view that philosophy and the other cognitive sciences have consistently gone wrong in this century by failing to see the importance of the human brain's ability to *consciously* represent the world. Hence, along with his positive theses about mind and language, Searle has defined himself by his opposition to four philosophical positions which fail to acknowledge consciousness: behaviorism and computationalism in the philosophy of mind, the causal theory of reference and indeterminacy of reference in the philosophy of language. Against behaviorism and computationalism, or what Searle refers to as "Strong artificial intelligence (AI)," Searle has offered the devastatingly influential *Chinese room argument*, which appears to show that computer programs cannot by themselves guarantee that the computers which run them will be able to understand, think, or have any other intentional mental state. Against the causal theory of reference, Searle has offered a set of arguments designed to show that words used by speakers refer not because of a causal connection to their referents, but rather due to the possession by the speaker of intentional states which pick out the referent from among all other objects. Similarly, Searle argues that Quine's thesis that the reference of words is ultimately indeterminate assumes behaviorism and cannot establish its conclusion without that assumption, an assumption which is no longer widely accepted.

More recently, Searle has confronted the relativist tradition flourishing outside of analytic philosophy. Against relativism - in the form of perspectivism, the view that our efforts to make sense of the world are separated into isolated perspectives, each unable to evaluate the others - Searle produces a set of arguments designed primarily to show this view presupposes the very commonsense realism about the world which it denies.

Searle's Milieu

It is impossible to understand Searle without understanding the behaviorist background against which he defined himself. Behaviorism is the thesis that only the correlations between stimuli and responses are worth studying and that the brain itself should be treated as a monolithic, closed black box. Behaviorism in both philosophy and psychology began in response to the failure of a previous school of thought. Prior to the current resurgence of interest in the conscious mind (which Searle's work has helped to bring on) the last serious psychological or philosophical theory which gave a place to the conscious mind was introspectionism, the chief defender of which was William James. Introspectionism flourished briefly at the end of the 1800s and the beginning of the 1900s. It was ultimately brought down by the failure of the introspectionists to convince others that their method was truly scientific. At the same time, there was a growing impatience in philosophy with the speculative metaphysical theories of the then ruling school, known as absolute idealism. These two trends combined to create a general belt-tightening mood in both disciplines. For its part, psychology opted for behaviorism of the stimulus-response variety. Here was real science: the stimuli and responses are all observable, and there are endless amounts of work to do cataloging the effects of different stimulus regimens, intensities, and so on. Philosophy chose positivism, the view that only claims whose means of

Intentionality

objective verification can be clearly stated are meaningful, something which supported behaviorism and ruled out introspective reports, along with metaphysics in general.[1]

Beginning in the 1930s, philosophers developed their own version of behaviorism, called logical, linguistic, or philosophical behaviorism. Logical behaviorism grew primarily out of the philosophy of language, when the philosophers Wittgenstein[2] and Ryle[3] developed analyses of mental verbs such as "see," "think," "know," and "remember." They argued that the proper way to analyze these terms was to observe how we applied them in ordinary life. Since I cannot see inside your mind, I discern whether or not you are seeing, remembering, understanding by your behavior. Each of these mental concepts has certain behavioral criteria which we look for when we apply them. These criteria, they contended, are much more relevant to the meanings of mental state words than any inchoate goings on in the mind.

Someone might object, however, that when I apply psychological terms to *myself* (e.g., "I am in pain") I certainly am not going by my behavior. Wittgenstein's response to this was to argue that when I say that I am in pain, I do not introspect my state of mind, apply a linguistic description to it, then voice this description to others. Rather, I simply give voice to my inner states with the same immediacy and naturalness that children do when they cry out in pain. Whatever happens, it is not a process of picking out an inner entity and applying a linguistic term to it. There are no public criteria for how to identify these inner entities, Wittgenstein further argued, so there is no way to distinguish between "It seems to me that x is occurring," where x is some mental state and "x is occurring" - not the sort of thing one can build a science on.

The positivists and the logical behaviorists share with Searle, however, the title "analytic philosopher." Analytic philosophy is the major philosophical movement in the English-speaking world in the 20th century. It is characterized by a reliance on logical techniques and the analysis of language and meaning. Analytic philosophy traces to the writings of Gottlob Frege, Bertrand Russell, G.E. Moore, and Wittgenstein at the beginning of the century. In his 1996 article "Contemporary Philosophy in the United States," Searle traces its roots back further:

> One can also see analytic philosophy as a natural descendant of the empiricism of the great British philosophers Locke, Berkeley and Hume, and of the transcendental philosophy of Kant.... It arose when the empiricist tradition in epistemology, together with the foundationalist enterprise of

Kant, were tied to the methods of logical analysis and the philosophical theories invented by Gottlob Frege in the late nineteenth century.[4]

A new field of philosophy, the philosophy of language, began with Frege and became for several periods throughout the 20th century the fastest-progressing and most influential branch of analytic philosophy. The philosophy of language conducted in this century can be seen as a debate between behaviorist approaches emphasizing our reliance on a person's behavior in using and interpreting language, and internalist approaches such as Searle's which emphasize the mental states running on behind the language behavior. In his landmark 1960 book, *Word and Object*,[5] W.V.O. Quine argued that what exactly someone means when she uses a word can never be determined for certain. In response to this, Searle argued in a 1987 article[6] that Quine came to the conclusion of indeterminacy by assuming that only information about the speaker's behavior and surroundings were relevant to determining her references, in short, by assuming behaviorism. There is a plain mental fact of what a person means by a word, Searle said, and this removes the indeterminacy, and makes meaning again a useful concept.

The behaviorist background, both in philosophy and psychology, against which Searle developed had an influence which most everyone now agrees was stifling. The relation between computationalism,[7] the other popular theory of the mind opposed by Searle, and behaviorism is complex. On the one hand, the development of artificial intelligence in the 1950s and 60s was vital to breaking the death grip of behaviorism. Now psychologists could talk about what went on inside the head because they had a theoretical framework for doing so: the computer model. However, computationalism continued to encourage the idea that the actual neurophysiological processes the brain employs to produce mental states are not relevant because, according to the computer metaphor of the mind, they are only the hardware of the computer. What is important is the program, or the formal set of rules or instructions that the processes embody. Programs can run on virtually any hardware, including silicon chips, so there is nothing special about the brain, the computationalists reasoned.

Biological Naturalism

In the place of behaviorism and computationalism, Searle offers a theory of the mind he refers to as *biological naturalism*, according to which the mind, consciousness, and intentionality are all biological phenomena. Many of the skeptical views about the mind such as behaviorism were designed specifically to avoid solving the mind-body problem, or the problem of how we can reconcile our apparently non-physical minds with our scientific picture of the world as consisting entirely of physical particles. Indeed, the mind-body problem is only a problem when we consider our conscious mental states. In contrast to the behaviorists, Searle attacks the mind-body problem squarely, offering a solution which fits neither of the standard categories: materialism, the view that the mind is entirely physical; nor dualism, the view that the mind consists of "mental stuff" or non-physical properties.

One of the most troubling aspects of consciousness is the way that the conscious states of each of us seem to be forever cut off from others. This seems to imply that, since mental events cannot be observed by more than one person, they cannot count as scientific facts. Searle's reply is to argue that this claim is mistaken, and that conscious events have genuine existence and should play an important role in our scientific theories of the mental, while acknowledging the claim that they are completely knowable only by the person who has them.

The distinction between what Searle and others refer to as the *first-person point of view* and the *third-person point of view* is crucial to this debate. This terminology is borrowed from linguistics: to speak in the first person is to speak about oneself using the word "I," while to speak in the third person is to speak about others using personal pronouns such as "he," or "she." When mental states are being ascribed these forms of speech indicate which point of view on a person's mental states is being taken. Someone attending to his own mental states is taking the first-person point of view, and accordingly will report what he learns by saying such things as "*I* am thinking about Kennedy." Our normal third-person point of view is of the behaving person from the outside. We might gain a third-person point of view of events inside your brain, by looking at your functional MRI for instance, but such views can never completely capture what is available to the first-person point of view, according to Searle.

Two of Searle's most important arguments rely on the first-person point of view for their force: the Chinese room argument, and the argument against Quine's indeterminacy thesis. Taken as a package,

Intentionality

the arguments from the first-person point of view provide a powerful message: consciousness and what goes on in it are important for our theories of mind and language. In passing, Searle has also made a methodological point: try testing out your theory of the mind or language from the first-person point of view. Unfortunately, the facts we learn about exclusively from the first-person point of view are difficult to express in impersonal, third-person techniques. This puts Searle in the position, with these arguments, of insisting that anyone can verify the fact in her own case. While philosophers have intensely examined the nature of the first-person point of view and the nature of the facts involved, and questioned the apparent incorrigibility of what is learned, Searle's success is testament to the robustness of consciousness. In order to clarify further the nature of the first-person point of view, Searle has taken up the challenge of examining consciousness in more recent work in which he describes and critiques the different introspectively detectable features of consciousness and reviews various scientific theories of consciousness.

In the place of relativism, Searle reacquaints us with plain old realism, the view that there exists a mind-independent world. Searle couples realism with other commonsense ontological views, such as the idea that we very often do know about the way things are in the world outside of us, and the correspondence theory of truth, the view that our thoughts and sentences are true if they correspond to the facts of the world. Several arguments which appear to show that realism is either incoherent or false do not actually do so, Searle contends. They fail to do this because their authors fail to realize that they are assuming the very thing they are claiming is incorrect - realism. Other arguments fail because they point out flaws in our knowledge gathering procedures (such as science), and conclude that knowledge is impossible. Against these Searle argues that such conclusions are far too sweeping.

Searle fits squarely in the analytic tradition, yet he is not a typical analytic philosopher. His writing does not resemble typical analytic philosophy, mainly in that it is extremely simple, and foregoes jargon almost entirely ("intentionality" itself is one of a few exceptions). Philosophers who write simply, however, and defend commonsense positions, run the risk of making it look as if they haven't done any work. After all, if you cannot say something other than what everyone believes, you haven't learned anything: everyone yawns or simply laughs when the philosopher succeeds in proving his own existence. Yet to be able to state philosophical problems and propose solutions in a way which makes the problem seem clear and the solution seem obvious takes huge amounts of work, far more work than leaving problems in their jargon-encased forms and simply assuming that any difficulty people have in understanding one's writing is due either to the fact that they are not experts, or to the difficulty of the problem itself. In *Mind, Language and Society* (1998), Searle says

> This book, then, may give the impression that I am taking you along a smooth and open road. That is an illusion. We are on a narrow path through a jungle. My method of exposition is to point out the path and then point to the parts of the jungle we need to avoid.[8]

Stating the obvious can itself be a sort of perfomative (see Chapter 2) in that it creates the obviousness of what is being pointed out:

> It is worth saying what sounds obvious because what seems obvious usually only seems that way after you have said it. Before you say it, it is not obvious what it is you need to say.[9]

Searle's philosophy is strongly argument-based, in the academic and legal sense of the term "an argument" which means roughly, "a reason." The Chinese room argument, for instance, is a reason to reject a certain view of the mind: the mind a computer program. Similarly, Searle marshals a set of reasons for why we should reject the form of relativism known as perspectivism. The arguments are presented very clearly as arguments, and this makes the challenge to whoever is being addressed quite clear. Searle prefers this argumentative style to the style of philosophical writing in which the philosopher tells a long story from the point of view of his theory, which the reader is impressed by the reasonableness of. Or worse, the hyperdense academic style with abbreviations for all the philosophical positions and their infinite amendments. Both of these alternative styles suffer from the fact that their complexities make the detection of errors extremely difficult. Searle's writing in general is completely unpretentious and is guided by the goal of expressing the arguments and objections clearly. Searle sees in his discussants, however, a deadly tendency to combine the counterintuitive quality of their views with an obfuscatory writing style:

> Authors who are about to say something that sounds silly very seldom come right out and say it. Usually a set of rhetorical or stylistic devices is employed to avoid having to say it in words of one syllable. The most obvious of these devices is to beat around the bush with a lot of evasive prose.[10]

Just as did Wittgenstein, who believed that certain philosophical positions were "diseases of thought," and that the role of the philosopher is both to refute them and to treat these diseases, minimally by making them explicit and offering alternative ways of thinking, Searle concerns himself with the methodologies and motives behind the positions of his interlocutors. He is often astonished at how unconcerned they are with how unintuitive their positions are. "Why is it," he wonders,

> that when we start doing philosophy we are almost inexorably driven to deny things that we all know to be true - for example, that there is a real world, that we can have certain sorts of knowledge of that world, that statements are typically true if they correspond to the facts in the world and false if they don't?[11]

As opposed to the curious reflexive tendency of the typical analytic philosopher to reject some aspect of our everyday views of the world, Searle's impulse and conscious decision is to save the default views, and oppose them only when an alternative theory is clearly superior, and the reasons and/or motives behind the mistake in our everyday view are clear. This is one reason why post-argument diagnosis of the malignant roots behind a philosophical position is important in Searle's view.

Intentional states

Thinking, seeing, understanding, being angry, being in pain, and feeling depressed are all mental states. *Intentional states* are those mental states which are about, or represent, features and events of the world. Thinking, seeing, and understanding are intentional states, because we are thinking about something, or seeing something, or understanding something to be the case. Most of the thoughts and images which flow through our minds during the day are about events in the world, for instance, when you remember the fall of the Berlin wall, your mental state is about that event. Other mental states, such as a depression not traceable to any particular event, lack intentionality. Simply seeing an object is also an example of an intentional state because your mental state is directed at the objects of perception.

The intentions which precede voluntary actions are also a type of intentional state in that they typically represent the agent and the world, but there is nothing special about them. This terminological accident confuses some into thinking either that intentionality refers solely to intentions and perhaps applies only to mental states directed at future states of affairs (e.g., I intend to win the prize), or that intentions hold a privileged status among their fellow intentional states, both of which are wrong.[12] Intentional states can be both conscious (e.g., seeing) or unconscious (e.g., a belief you have but are not currently thinking about), but even the unconscious ones must have the capacity to become conscious. Searle refers to this claim as the connection principle. We will examine it in Chapter 3: *Mind*.

Satisfaction Conditions, Intentional Content, and Aspectual Shapes

When I form a belief say, that Caesar crossed the Rubicon, the belief represents the world as being a certain way. If that belief in fact fits the way the world is, then the belief is true, or more generally, *satisfied*. When I have a desire or intention, alternatively, I want the world to fit, or satisfy, my intentional state. Intentional states can be categorized into two basic types: those with mind-to-world direction of fit, such as belief (I want my beliefs to fit the world) and those with world-to-mind direction of fit, such as desire (I want the world to fit my desires). The broader concept of satisfaction fits both desires and beliefs; a belief is satisfied when it fits reality. If my belief is not satisfied, I change my belief, if my desire is not satisfied, I try to change the world.

Intentional states all have an *intentional content*, which specifies the exact conditions under which the belief is true or the desire is satisfied. Intentional states specify their content under what Searle calls *aspectual shapes*. When an intentional state represents an object, it represents it in some ways, some aspects, and not in some others; this is a feature of all representation. For instance, a person can desire water but not desire H_2O. Vision always represents objects to us in certain ways. We see objects from a certain point of view, and as having certain properties. Applied to entire intentional states, the state represents its conditions of satisfaction under certain aspects and not others. For instance, I will not consider my desire to be the best ocarina player in the world to be satisfied if I find that I am the *only* ocarina player in the world.

Aspectual shapes are representations of properties of objects or states of affairs. A visual intentional state, for example, might contain an aspectual shape that represents an object as being green, and another aspectual shape which represents the object as being spherical. Given that objects have a potentially infinite number of properties, there are an equally large number of aspectual shapes, since every property of an object allows for the creation of an aspectual shape that represents that property. As far as the ontological status of aspectual shapes themselves, they are properties of the brain, according to Searle, but properties which only that particular brain's owner can ever know completely (more on this in Chapter 3).

One way to determine what the conditions of satisfaction of an intentional state are is to see what, according to the agent, would or would not satisfy that intentional state. The term "satisfaction conditions" is also "harmlessly ambiguous," says Searle, in that it can mean either the abstract specification of the content of an intentional state, or the real world events which satisfy that intentional state when they come into being.[13] Thus if I desire to own a horse, we can specify the (abstract) satisfaction conditions verbally as "that I own a horse," or we can say that the actual physical event of my taking ownership of the horse is the (concrete) satisfaction condition of that desire. Searle also uses the classical notion of an *intentional object*, but those are simply the objects in the world that our intentional states are about.

The words in the sentence "John Searle was born in Denver" also possess intentionality, in that they are about something in the world, a philosopher named John Searle. However, it is an important tenet of Searle's philosophy that the intentionality which words possess is *derived* from the intentionality present in the human mind, which Searle calls *intrinsic* intentionality. Humans confer intentionality on words; without this what you are looking at is merely a bunch of ink stains on paper. We confer intentionality on words by imposing conditions of satisfaction on them. Awareness of the intrinsic/derived distinction is important for understanding Searle's attempt to show that computers do not possess intentional states (more exactly, Searle's conclusion is: running a computer program is not sufficient to produce an intentional state, see Chapter 3). The intentionality present in the output of a computer program, for instance, a correct answer to a question, is derived from the intrinsic intentionality present in the mind of the person interpreting the output, as well as the mind of the person who wrote the program.

Perception and Intentional Causation

Perception is an intentional state, with mind-to-world direction of fit. When I visually perceive something, say a red car, that intentional state has conditions of satisfaction, primarily that there really is a red car there in front of me. Hence we may state the intentional content of the experience as:

> I have a visual experience (that there is a red car there).

When I see something I also assume that my current visual experience is at least partly caused by that thing. So the intentional content is more adequately specified as:

> I have a visual experience (that there is a red car there, and the existence of a red car there is causing this visual experience).

Thus, there is an element of self-referentiality in the intentional content of the visual state: the content refers to the visual experience itself. This self-referential condition might be violated, for instance, in a case where a scientist has implanted electrodes in my brain which produce a vivid simulation of reality. In such a case, I might be in a state quite similar to the normal one in which I see a red car, but as long as I know that the experience is being caused by the electrodes and not by the fact that there is a red car in front of me, I am not in the same intentional state as when I really see the red car, because the causal self-referentiality is missing. If I forget, however, that my experience is caused by the electrodes and come to mistake my virtual reality for reality, then it is possible for me to be in the same intentional state as the person who really sees a red car. The difference between us then is that my intentional state is not satisfied, while hers is.

The tracking of causal relations is an important property of intentional states. They are exquisitely sensitive to how they are caused, as well as what they can cause. Searle says that:

> Our minds are also in constant causal contact with the world. When we see things, the objects we see cause our visual experiences of them. When we remember events in our past, those past events cause our present memories. When we intend to move our bodies, those intentions cause the bodily movements.[14]

What Searle calls intentional causation also involves intentional content that is self-referential. When we want something, that wanting itself plays a causal role in getting us the thing we want. These are cases in which intentional states both cause and represent their conditions of satisfaction. For instance, if I desire to own a sheepdog, that desire both represents me owning a sheepdog, and causes me to buy the sheepdog, that is, it causes my ownership of the sheepdog. When we intend to move body parts, self-referential conditions of satisfaction come into play. When I intend to extend my leg, the intention has more in its conditions of satisfaction than just that I actually do extend my leg. It also contains the condition that it must be the *intention* that causes the leg to extend. When we describe any rational human behavior, we are employing the notion of intentional causation. This explains why behaviorism failed in its attempt to describe human behavior in nonmentalistic terms, according to Searle.

The Network, and the Background, of Intentionality

Our beliefs and other intentional states all fit together into a densely interconnected, holistic network. Each intentional state requires a large number of other intentional states in order to have the role in the person's psychology that it does. One way to see this is try to imagine a being with only one (or a few) intentional states, and see that this is impossible. Suppose a devout Yankees fan teaches his infant son to say, "The Yankees are the best," as his first sentence. Does the son have the intentional state, the belief, that the Yankees are the best team? In order to have this belief, he would have to know that the Yankees are a baseball team, that they compete with other teams, that being the best team means winning the World Series, and so on, none of which he knows. He fails to have this intentional state because his network of intentional states is not sufficiently developed to support it.

The network of intentional states rests on a set of more basic abilities that allow intentional states to be formed and to have real effects on the world. Searle refers to this set of abilities as the *background*.[15] The background is the set of nonrepresentational mental capacities which allow the mind to represent the world. For instance, the intention to withdraw some money from an ATM only functions as a representation against a background of a large number of abilities we have, such as the ability to press the buttons and read the little video screen. Without these abilities it makes little sense to have such an intention. The background forms the interface between intentional states and the world, determining both the way our intentional states are causally affected by the world, and the way they causally affect the world. In the case of perception, our background abilities allow us to sense the world in several different modalities, and form perceptual intentional states on the basis of this, whereas in the case of action, our background abilities allow us to negotiate with the external world in all its variety in order to satisfy our intentions and desires.

Searle divides the background into two parts, the *deep background* and the *local background*. The deep background includes capacities common to all normal human beings in virtue of their biological makeup - capacities such as walking, eating, grasping, perceiving, recognizing, and the preintentional stance that takes account of the solidity of things, and the independent existence of objects and other people.[16]

The local background includes skills we learn as part of learning to live in our particular culture, such as how to open a door, how to drive a car, and how to behave in culturally acceptable ways.

One argument which Searle gives for the existence of background abilities is to show them at work in our understanding of the literal meaning of certain sentences.[17] Consider several literal uses of the verb "cut" in the commands, "Cut the grass," "Cut the cake," "Cut the cloth," and "Cut your skin." We need to interpret "cut" differently in each case, as evidenced by the fact that one would not be understanding the commands correctly if one ran a lawn mower over the cake, or tried to cut the lawn with a scalpel. The reason why we understand all of these utterances in the proper way is that we have experience with each of those kinds of cutting; this experience is embodied in our background abilities.

It is difficult to describe exactly what our epistemic relation is to certain background presuppositions. We are not normally conscious of the background, but when we reflect on it, we tend to artificially treat its elements as if they themselves are intentional states:

> Eating lunch in a restaurant, I am surprised when I lift my mug of beer by its near weightlessness. Inspection reveals that the thick mug is not glass but plastic. We would naturally say I *believed* that the mug was made of glass, and I *expected* it to be heavy. But that is wrong.[18]

The background is part of what allows our mental states to have intentionality, but it itself does not consist of intentional states:

> As the precondition of Intentionality, the Background is as invisible to Intentionality as the eye which sees is invisible to itself.[19]

Another rather obvious reason why the background cannot itself be intentional is that this claim threatens to produce an infinite regress: what is it that makes the background intentional? One way to describe our relation to propositions such as the one expressed by "This glass is solid," is to say that we are committed to the truth of them, at least in the sense that it would be inconsistent with our behavior to deny them.[20]

One challenge likely to be put to the hypothesis of the background increasingly as we come to learn more about the brain is that what Searle describes as background abilities actually do involve representations, but representations of a special sort, known as *analog representations*. These approaches acknowledge the wrongness of saying that Searle *believed* that the glass was heavy, since beliefs are not normally a form of analog representation, while still insisting that the person *represents* the mug as being heavy. The brain's preferred mode of analog representation is the topographic map. These maps represent adjacent portions of what is represented with spatially adjacent areas, the same way that a map of a state represents the fact that two cities are near by putting them near each other on the map. The somatotopic maps which represent the body generally have the same look and structure as the body itself, so that points of the body which are near are represented by parts of the map which are nearby. The occipital lobe organizes much of its visual information into what are called retinotopic maps: this means that adjacent areas of the eye's retina are represented by adjacent areas on the map.

Searle gives an example of a problematic epistemic state, which we are not sure is a belief or not.[21] Suppose I were to enter my office one day and find a huge chasm in the floor. I would be surprised, but now does this mean that I believe that my office floor is solid, or worse, that I have a belief that there is no chasm in the middle of my office floor? We get a robust intuition that there is something wrong in ascribing such beliefs. Perhaps this is because, while I do represent my office floor as solid, I represent this in analog form, rather than in the form of explicit belief. I have been in my office hundreds of times, and my brain has constructed a detailed analog representation of the room. It is this representation which is not satisfied when I see the chasm.

The main block to bringing analog contents under the theoretical apparatus of intentional states is that there is as yet no working, general account of satisfaction, or fitting, for them. This may be a case where we discern how the brain judges fit before we develop a theory of it. *Map*, of course, is an intentional concept; it is not clear that we should be calling them that. Another way to put this is to ask whether their intentionality intrinsic, or derived. As we will see in Chapter 3, this question depends partly on what relation the alleged maps have to consciousness.

Endnotes

[1] The classic work of positivism is A.J. Ayer's *Language, Truth, and Logic*, London: Gallancz, 1946.

[2] See Wittgenstein's *The Blue and Brown Books*, New York, Harper and Row, 1958, and *Philosophical Investigations*, New York: MacMillan Publishing Co. Inc., 1953.

[3] See Ryle's *The Concept of Mind*, New York: Barnes and Noble, Inc., 1949.

[4] "Contemporary Philosophy in the United States," in *The Blackwell Companion to Philosophy*, eds. Nicholas Bunnin and E.P. Tsui-James, Oxford: Blackwell Publishers Ltd., 1996.

[5] Cambridge, Mass.: The MIT Press; and New York: Wiley.

[6] "Indeterminacy, Empiricism, and the First Person," *Journal of Philosophy*, **LXXXIV**, pp. 123-146.

[7] I use the term "computationalism" to refer to both Strong artificial intelligence and Turing machine functionalism. See Chapter 3.

[8] *Mind, Language and Society*, New York: Basic Books, 1998, p. 9.

[9] *Ibid.*, p. 9.

[10] *The Rediscovery of the Mind*, Cambridge, Mass.: The M.I.T. Press, 1992, p. 4.

[11] *Mind, Language, and Society*, p. 9.

[12] See *Intentionality*, p. 5.

[13] *Ibid.*, p. 13.

[14] *Mind, Language, and Society*, pp. 104-105, see also Chapter 4 of *Intentionality*.

[15] For more information about the background, see *Intentionality*, Chapter 5; *The Rediscovery of the Mind*, Chapter 8; and *Mind, Language, and Society*, pp. 107-109.

[16] *Intentionality*, pp. 143-144.

[17] See *The Rediscovery of the Mind*, pp. 178-179; see also *Intentionality*, pp. 144-148.

[18] *Intentionality*, p. 157.

[19] *Ibid.*, p. 157.

[20] *The Rediscovery of the Mind*, p. 185.

[21] *Intentionality*, p. 155.

2
Language

In all discussions in the philosophy of language and the philosophy of mind, it is absolutely essential at some point to remind oneself of the first-person case.

"Indeterminacy, Empiricism, and the First Person," 1987

Introduction

How do the sounds coming out of our mouths and the lines we make on paper come to have meaning, or come to be classifiable as true or false? Searle's answer is that we perform what he calls *speech acts*, by imposing conditions of satisfaction and imposing intentionality on the words we say or write. Words do not refer all by themselves, speakers make them refer, with a special kind of activity we humans have perfected.

There are several connecting links between intentionality in mind and intentionality in language in Searle's philosophy, including the notion of aspectual shape. The aspectual shape of an intentional state is the particular *way* we represent our object of interest. Some of our aspectual shapes are linguistic, for instance in the case of the woman who desires water but does not desire H_2O. This is a case in which the primarily mental phenomenon of aspectual shape also gives rise to linguistic phenomena, such as the one known as intensionality, or opacity. A report of an intentional state is said to be opaque when substitution of co-referential terms (that is, terms which refer to the same object) affects the truth-value of the sentence. If Jill does not know that what she calls "water" is also H_2O, the following substitution affects the truth value of the sentence:

Jill desires water.
Water is H_2O.

Therefore, Jill desires H_2O.

According to Searle, it is important to understand such linguistic phenomena as more general phenomena studied by the philosophy of mind. Human linguistic capacities augment and piggyback on the basic intentionality which we posses whether we know a language or not. The intentionality of the mind is the cause of the intentionality of written or spoken words. This is one of the main reasons why Searle argues that the philosophy of language comes under the more general heading of the philosophy of mind. One reason why Searle is careful to make this clear is that there is a strong trend in analytic philosophy in the other direction. Many philosophers come to the philosophy of mind from the philosophy of language, for instance by moving from an examination of the semantic properties of sentences which report beliefs to the question of the ontology of beliefs themselves. The problem of opacity - that is, the problem of saying exactly why arguments such as the one above fail - is intractable as long as we try to understand the phenomenon as a purely linguistic one, and fail to see it as ultimately a problem in the philosophy of mind, Searle would argue.[1]

Speech Acts

Searle's book *Speech Acts* (1969) details his views on the central issues in the philosophy of language. The book grew out of Searle's 1959 doctoral dissertation at Oxford. While at Oxford, Searle was strongly influenced by his teacher, the British philosopher John Austin, and much of Searle's early work commented on and augmented Austin's. Born in 1911, Austin's tenure at Oxford lasted nine years, from 1952 until his early death in 1960. His work was marked by a commonsensical approach coupled with fine-grained analyses of the meanings of certain words crucial to philosophical problems, such as "pretend," "illusion," or "excuse." Austin emphasized the idea that using words was *doing* something, performing an action. According to Searle, this emphasis opened up a new view of the philosophy of language, contrary to the traditional view that it belongs more with the study of logic and formal semantics:

> One great merit of Austin's theory of speech acts is that it enabled subsequent philosophers to construe the philosophy of language as a branch of the philosophy of action. Since speech acts are as much actions as any other actions, the philosophical analysis of language is part of the general analysis of human behavior. And since intentional human

behavior is an expression of mental phenomena, it turns out that the philosophy of language and the philosophy of action are really just different aspects of one larger area, namely, the philosophy of mind.[2]

It is important to be clear, however, about Searle's relationship to the school associated with Austin, known as ordinary language philosophy, whose methods also traced to the work of Gilbert Ryle, and Wittgenstein. This school was characterized by the idea that philosophical problems can be solved (or seen to no longer be problems) merely by examining the way in which words are normally used. For instance, in order to answer questions about knowledge, an ordinary language philosopher would examine the conditions under which we apply the word "know" in everyday life. While Searle accepted some of the ideas and techniques of these philosophers, he was never an ordinary language philosopher, preferring to augment their methods with more general techniques from other philosophical schools.

Austin referred to the making of statements, the asking of questions, the making of requests and so on, as *illocutionary acts*.[3] Searle points out that there are several important isomorphisms between these speech acts and intentional states. Principally, just as any intentional state is both a state of a certain type and has a certain content (e.g., believing that New York will win the World Series, and wishing that New York will win the World Series, are two different intentional state types with the same content), speech acts of different types can have the same content. For instance, Will you eat your beets? Please eat your beets; and You will eat your beets, are speech acts of different types (question, request, command), but with the same content. These and other similarities between speech acts and intentional states allowed Searle to apply much of the theoretical apparatus of intentional states to the philosophy of language.

The word "meaning" itself has several meanings, but there are two primary senses which philosophers focus on: word meaning and speaker meaning. The word "links" in German, for instance, means "left" in English; this is an example of word meaning. Words have meanings as part of a language, and the meaning of a sentence is determined partly by these word meanings, in addition to the rules of syntax. Speaker's meaning, on the other hand, is a matter of what the speaker intends a word to mean, and hence can deviate from word meaning. Searle's analysis of meaning focuses on speaker meaning: When a speaker makes a meaningful utterance, he is imposing conditions of satisfaction on the sounds he makes:

> The key to understanding meaning is this: meaning is a form of derived intentionality. The original or intrinsic intentionality of a speaker's thought is transferred to words, sentences, marks, symbols, and so on.[4]

The Description Theory of Reference vs. the Causal Theory

How do proper names, such as "Bertrand Russell," and "The Grand Coulee Dam," refer to that person and that object when a speaker utters them? What exactly is the nature of the connection between the name and the object? This is a specific form of an important and more general question: How does language connect to the world? There are at present two main competing theories of reference, the *description theory*, which Searle's approach is a variant of, and the *causal theory* of Putnam[5] and Kripke.[6]

The Description Theory of Names

It is important to understanding this debate to understand the connection between what certain causal theorists call propositions, and what Searle calls intentional contents. Classically, propositions are the meanings of sentences, so that the three sentences "Es regnet," "Il pleut," and "It is raining" express the same proposition. Or, in Searle's terminology, they have the same conditions of satisfaction, i.e., the same intentional content. Propositions and intentional contents are both held to be the relevant truth bearers for sentences and intentional states, so that Searle's intentional contents can be viewed as his candidate for what propositions are. One opposing camp, which has tended to be paired with the causal theory lately, holds that propositions are concrete states of affairs (i.e., what Searle would call conditions of satisfaction, in the concrete sense of the term). Hence, the debate between Searle and the externalists can also be seen as a debate about whether propositions are mental, or "concrete."

It is worth looking briefly at Gottlob Frege's theory of proper names, since Searle's theory is a descendant of it. On the Fregean account declarative sentences express what he calls *thoughts* which have as their constituents *ways of thinking* of the references of the sentence's terms and predicates; thoughts are Frege's propositions,

Frege's ways of thinking (or *senses*) correspond to Searle's aspectual shapes. The words of the sentence can also be used to refer to these ways of thinking. In the case of belief attributions, declarative sentences occurring as content sentences (e.g., the "S" in "a believes that S") express the thought which is being attributed. According to Frege, the content sentences of attributions also *indirectly refer* to the thought being attributed. For instance, in the belief attribution sentence "Tom believes that the tallest spy is standing," the content sentence "the tallest spy is standing," indirectly refers to a thought which has as its constituents a way of thinking of the tallest spy (indirectly referred to by "the tallest spy"), together with a way of thinking of the property of standing (indirectly referred to by "is standing").

Frege's technical term for a way of thinking is *sense*. In Frege's theory, senses have the following properties:

1. They are thoughts, and the constituents of thoughts.

2. They pick out their references uniquely. Very roughly, our grasp of the senses of words which we hear is what allows us to know what is being referred to. On the standard interpretation of Frege, this has been taken to imply that senses of singular terms (such as proper names) can typically be linguistically expressed by the form 'the [delta]' where [delta] is a set of descriptions which, taken jointly, are true only of a single individual.

3. They account for the potential informativeness of certain identity sentences. The reason why a = b, where "a" and "b" are different singular terms, can be informative, whereas b = b cannot be, is that "a" and "b" have different associated senses.

There are other senses which pick out the tallest spy, expressible with different singular terms, but these yield different thoughts. For instance, if the tallest spy is named "Ortcutt," we might assert "Tom believes that Ortcutt is standing," and so attribute the following belief object: (Ortcutt, is standing). That this is a different thought from (The tallest spy, is standing) is due to Frege's epistemic criterion of difference:

> If any agent can take different attitudes (e.g., belief and disbelief, or belief and 'abstention' or indifference) to the thoughts expressed by sentences S and S', then S and S' express different thoughts.

So for instance, Tom might believe that Ortcutt is standing, yet not believe that the tallest spy is standing, if he doesn't know that Ortcutt is the tallest spy. According to Frege, then, the content sentences "Ortcutt is standing" and "The tallest spy is standing" indirectly refer to different thoughts.

The concept equivalent in Searle's philosophy to Fregean sense is aspectual shape. Unlike Fregean senses - which are abstract - Searle's aspectual shapes are psychological entities; they are properties of mental states. Frege says that thoughts are part of a common treasure which is transmitted from generation to generation, and that "the truth of a thought is timeless," and this is typically taken (along with other evidence) to indicate that Fregean senses and thoughts are abstract, in the sense of not having spatiotemporal properties. Frege is quite clear that thoughts and senses are not psychological entities; they are also sharable, in that it is possible for two people to think of something under the same sense.[7] As we will see in Chapter 3, aspectual shapes are a special type of property in Searle's philosophy, since they can only be known by one person - the person's in whose mind they exist. When Searle says, "the aspectual shape must matter to the agent,"[8] this is his version of Frege's epistemic criterion of difference for senses. Similarly, Frege's thoughts are equivalent to Searle's intentional states.

The description theory traces to Frege's theory of *sense*, but the version which Searle defends would be more aptly named the internalist theory. The stereotypical description theorist is held to believe that a speaker is able to refer because there is in his mind a description which fits the referent uniquely. So, I can refer to Aristotle because I know that he fits the descriptions "pupil of Plato," and "teacher of Alexander." The idea that there is in the mind of the speaker a linguistic entity - a description - is far too narrow according to Searle. Sometimes the only grasp a speaker has on the referent is an ability to recognize it, as when a child learns a proper name before learning any descriptions true of an object.[9] What is required for reference is that the object satisfy the intentional content in the mind of speaker. Any descriptions in the mind of the speaker are one type of intentional content.

The description theorist's idea that the speaker must have a certain amount of knowledge of the referent before she can refer to it has intuitive appeal. We might imagine a physicist who teaches his child to say "$E=mc^2$" instead of "Dada" as her first words. But when the baby says this, we do not believe that she is referring to energy, or that she believes that it is equal to mass multiplied by the speed of light squared. And this is precisely because we know that she does not know enough about these things to refer to them or have beliefs about them.

The Causal Theory of Names

As with many of the disputes Searle is involved in, this one comes down to a debate between Searle, arguing that reference is determined by internal, mental conditions, and the other side, arguing that reference is determined by external, non-mental factors. According to the causal theory, reference succeeds when there is a causal chain of the appropriate kind connecting the speaker's use of a name with the bearer of that name. Thus when you say "Aristotle," your use of that name traces, via a long causal chain, back into time until it reaches Aristotle himself. That causal chain was initiated when Aristotle's mother first named him, an act the causal theorists refer to as the *initial baptism*. The difference between the two theories does not turn on causality, since Searle also believes that certain causal relations are important, for instance between an object we see and our conscious visual state. It is part of the intentional content for such visual states that the objects themselves are causing the visual intentional state.

This basic form of the causal theory needs to be augmented with a further condition, however. Surprisingly enough, this further condition is a clause concerning the *intentions* the speaker must have in using the name. When someone learns of a name and then uses it, he must intend to use the name to refer to the same person that his teacher used it to refer to.[10] To see why this is so, consider the case of a man who walks past a classroom and hears the teacher say "the philosopher Aristotle." When someone asks him later what the professor was talking about, he says, "he was talking about Aristotle." Has the eavesdropper referred to Aristotle? The causal theorist would say that he has, because a causal chain runs from Aristotle, through the professor, to the eavesdropper, and the eavesdropper intends to use the name in the same way that the professor did. Suppose further, though, that when the eavesdropper gets home, he decides to name his new kitten Aristotle. Then when he calls "Aristotle!" to the kitten, is he referring to the philosopher? It doesn't seem so, and even though the casual chain is still there - he learned the name from the professor - the intentional criterion is not met, however, because he does not intend to use the name to refer to the person that the professor was referring to.

The existence of this internal, intentional criterion often comes as a surprise to those who think that the dispute is between a purely internal theory such as Searle's and a purely external theory, the causal theory. Searle capitalizes on its inclusion, arguing that the causal theory secures referential links primarily from this condition about the speaker's intentions, i.e., from an intentional state.[11]

Objections to the Searle's Theory and Their Responses

The Twin Earth Argument

Imagine that there is a planet exactly like Earth far away on the other side of the Milky Way - call it Twin Earth. Twin Earth is so far away from Earth that there is no real causal interaction between the two planets. Twin Earth, however, is eerily similar to Earth. On Twin Earth, the President is also someone named Clinton, who has all of the properties of our President Clinton here on earth. There could be then, a person on earth and his twin on Twin Earth (call them Tom and Twin Tom) who have exactly the same intentional content, for instance, that he is the President and that he is married to someone named Hillary. The problem for the description theory, according to Putnam, is that their intentional contents are equally satisfied by either Clinton or Twin Clinton. Hence the description theory does not necessarily attach their uses of the name "President Clinton" to the right people. The causal theory, on the other hand, seems to give the desired result, since Tom is causally connected to Clinton in the appropriate way, and Twin Tom is similarly connected to Twin Clinton.

Searle's response to this is to argue that the intentional content behind the use of the name has a self-referentiality similar to that which we saw in Chapter 1 is contained in the intentional content of perceptual states. One of the satisfaction conditions of my seeing a red car is that *my* visual experience actually be caused by the red car. Similarly, by "Clinton," Tom means, "the person *I* have heard and read referred to as Clinton."[12] Tom would not have heard or read about Twin Clinton, so this seems to be a way in which the intentional content of the two Toms can single out the right objects.

The Two Patches Argument[13]

Suppose a man volunteers for a psychology experiment. He is seated in a room where two identical red patches are projected on the wall in front of him, one on top of the other. He calls the one on top "A" and the one on the bottom "B." Seemingly, the only identifying description he can associate with the name "A" is that it is "the one on top." But, unbeknownst to the man, the experimenters have switched his normal glasses with inverting glasses, so that the one on top is actually the one on the bottom. Hence this appears to be a case where the intentional content "the one on top" is not satisfied in spite of the reference, to the square which is actually on the bottom, still being successful.

As before, Searle's strategy in reply is to point out that the intentional contents of the person involved are richer than might first appear. The self-referentiality of perception is at work here again: The man's intentional content for the patch on top also includes the requirement that it be the one causing his experience of the square on top. Since the bottom square is actually causing his experience, it is the one he is referring to; this more powerful condition overides the description "the one on top" in fixing the reference of "A." This is another case in which Searle's philosophy can respond to an example which the stereotype description theory cannot, primarily because Searle has taken into account certain types of causal relations between our referents and our mental states, and the ability of these states to keep track of these causal relations.

The Modal Argument

On Frege's theory of sense, the description that a speaker associates with a particular name provides the definition of that name. The problem with this is that this seems to make certain statements analytically true (or true by definition) - statements which appear to be contingent. Thus if a speaker associates the description "the teacher of Alexander" with Aristotle, and that description is the definition of "Aristotle," this would make the sentence "Aristotle is the teacher of Alexander" analytically true. Similarly, we do not want the claim that Aristotle did not teach Alexander to be analytically false, in the way that "Bachelors are married" is. "Aristotle is the teacher of Alexander," seems to be a contingent statement, in that it seems quite possible that Aristotle never encountered Alexander.

Searle's response is to point out that the relation between the description associated with a name and the name is much weaker than that of definition. He adheres to what is known as the "cluster concept" version of the description theory, where no one particular description is necessarily associated with Aristotle. Aristotle needs to have at least some of the properties normally associated with him, but there is no one property which he must have.

Language Use, From the Inside, and From the Outside

One way to make sense of the debate between Searle and the externalist, causal theory is to see the two sides as having their intuitive basis in two different ways we naturally tend to conceive of what speakers are doing when they refer. We sometimes consider the speaker from the outside, as connected to his referent via an external causal chain. Other times we consider the situation from inside the speaker as it were. We pretend to be him, referring, and ask ourselves "If I knew what he knew, would I be referring?" To see this, consider the example of someone who, in the near future, goes to a business where one pays an hourly fee to put on a special helmet and suit which produces extremely vivid virtual reality illusions. Since he is a fan of former President Kennedy, he selects an illusion in which he will seem to be speaking with Kennedy in the Oval Office of the White House. The setup is not quite perfected to the point where they can provide a realistic simulation of a person, so one of the workers, Ralph, who is an expert on Kennedy, must put on another virtual reality suit and play the role of Kennedy. As the simulation progresses, the man gets more and more convinced by it and eventually comes to believe that he is in fact speaking to Kennedy. As the discussion in the Oval Office concludes, the man moves forward to shake hands. As he reaches out and says, "Great talking with you," how do we say who he is reaching toward and referring to? Is he reaching toward Kennedy, or toward Ralph? Does "you" refer to Kennedy, or to Ralph? The answer is, it depends. It depends on whether you are taking the external perspective, in which case he is referring to Ralph, even though he doesn't know it, or the internal perspective, in which he is referring to JFK. The causal theory takes the external point of view as intuitively basic, whereas Searle takes the internal point of view as his foundation. Perhaps rather than trying to emphasize one of these points of view at the expense of the other, a future theory will focus its efforts on understanding why our uses of language so readily make use of either one, and why we have evolved ways of using language which use both, and easily move from one to the other.

Against Quinean Indeterminacy

Suppose you are a linguist who has been sent to translate into English the language of a stone-age tribe living deep in the jungles of Borneo. You and a philosopher friend arrive in Borneo, locate the tribe, and as best you can given the language barrier, befriend them. The next morning you and your friend go out with some of the hunters in order to listen to and watch them, so that you can begin to learn their language. You have not been out long when a rabbit hops out of the brush into plain view. One of the hunters spots it and says to his fellow tribesman quietly, "Gavagai." You open your notebook and write

Language

"gavagai" = "rabbit." Your philosopher friend watches as you do this, however, and says, "Are you *sure* that 'gavagai' means 'rabbit'?" "Of course," you say, "what else could it mean?" "Well, it could mean 'undetached rabbit part', or 'time slice of a rabbit'," your friend replies. Your first inclination is to dismiss this as philosophical hair-splitting, but on second thought, you must admit that your friend has a point.

Quine claimed that there is nothing in the behavior of the natives (or in their surrounding environment) which can definitively answer the question of whether the hunter means "rabbit" or "undetached rabbit part." It is important to the example that the speakers are natives, we are not one of the tribe, so we are observing them as an outsider. In considering only the external behavior of the natives, Quine was influenced by the reigning theory in psychology, known as behaviorism. Behaviorists argue that only external, observable behavior of an organism is allowable as data. Introspection is notoriously unreliable, argue the behaviorists, and not at all well understood.

In his response to Quine, Searle argued for two things. First that there is a simple fact, which speakers are aware of, about what they means by a term. This is a fact about the speaker's brain, which would make it a biological fact, on Searle's view. Second, Searle argued that the apparent indeterminacy proved not, as Quine argued, that reference is indeterminate and mysterious, but that behaviorism is an incorrect paradigm for psychology, especially where the making and grasping of word references is concerned.[14] The view that mental states are not relevant to a scientific theory of language is, according to Searle,

> linguistic behaviorism with a vengeance. It has often been criticized and, in my view, often refuted, for example, by Noam Chomsky in his review of B.F. Skinner.[15] On one construal, my Chinese room argument can also be interpreted as a refutation. One way to refute this version of extreme linguistic behaviorism . . . would be to offer a *reductio ad absurdum* of its premises; and, indeed, it seems to me that Quine has offered one such famous *reductio*. If behaviorism were true, certain distinctions known independently to be valid would be lost.[16]

Reductio ad absurdum, or reduction to absurdity, is an ancient argument form in which a view is refuted, not directly by showing it to be false, but indirectly, by showing that something which the view implies is false or absurd. If behaviorism implies that we can never determine what someone is referring to by using a certain word, then this should cast doubt on behaviorism, not on the obvious fact that reference is determinate in the great majority of cases.

Searle's assertion that he knows what he is and is not referring to is similar to his assertion that it is a simple fact that he does not understand Chinese, in the Chinese room (see Chapter 3). It does seem that we are aware of what we are referring to when we use a word, although what exactly we are aware of is a difficult question. We also seem to be aware of different things while using the same word with the same reference. We know what we are referring to, but claims to knowledge invite the question, "How do you know?," and there is no obvious, general answer to this question in the case of reference. Having an image in one's mind of a rabbit is of course subject to the same sorts of indeterminacies which the sight of the actual rabbit was subject to: The picture might be either a picture of a rabbit or a picture of an undetached rabbit part. One sort of response Searle would give to the question of how we know is to say that our knowledge of what we are referring to is non-inferential, and this explains why we are not able to point to the basis of an inference - there was no such inference. There are some things we simply know.

When linguists actually do try to translate completely foreign languages into English, they do not practice behaviorism. According to Searle, the linguist

> tries to figure out what is going on in the mind of the native speaker, even at the level of particular words. And he can do this because he presupposes that he shares with the speaker of the exotic language a substantial amount of the Network and Background.[17]

It is our background capacities that rule out the bizarre possibilities of reference, such as "undetached rabbit part," because those capacities reflect what we are interested in and what we normally do.

In his post-argument diagnosis, Searle argued that Quine confused an epistemic issue with a semantic one. Semantic issues are about what makes sentences true. What makes a claim about what I am referring to true are certain features of my brain, more specifically, certain features of my intentional states. The question of how other people can come to know about those features is an epistemic issue, which is of secondary importance in determining reference, on Searle's approach.

Questions

Doesn't the Wittgenstein's Private Language Argument Rule Out What Searle is Trying to Do?

The private language argument is directed against the idea that the meaning of a word is the thing it refers to. Wittgenstein's 1952 book *Philosophical Investigations*[18] is a sustained attack on this theory. The private language argument is addressed at a specific subcase of the theory, the claim that the meaning of mental terms is the introspectively observable referent. The reason why there cannot be a private language about mental events is that, since there is only one person involved, there is no intersubjective agreement about word reference. When the person *thinks* the mental event is occurring again, there is no way to check him.

One of Wittgenstein's stipulations about the private language, however, is that it must refer to entities known only to the agent "so another person cannot understand the language."[19] So, the private language argument is specifically about the question of reference to introspectively observable events, not to public entities such as rabbits. The language of the natives is not a private one. The intentional contents which Searle uses to disambiguate references are not (as in the private language argument) what is being referred to. Rather, they are what determine reference to objects, according to Searle.

Can the Indeterminacy Be Removed From the Third-person Point of View Also?

Is Searle right in claiming that the fact of what exactly someone means by a word is locked inside her head; that we couldn't at some point in the future be able to access this fact from the third-person point of view? If it is true both that there is something in the mind or brain which determines what someone is referring to, and that those facts are only accessible to consciousness in a rather seamless, non-inferential way, perhaps we can get a better grasp on what the facts are by examining the brain from the third-person point of view.

Consider the following scenario: In the near future we find a part of the brain which is active when people speak, which we come to be convinced is where their *concepts* are. When we stimulate a certain part of this area, the conscious subject says: "Oranges, I was thinking about oranges, and an image of an orange came into my mind." We find that there are thousands of clearly demarcated areas, which we hypothesize are the person's different concepts. Furthermore, while there seem to be some systematic relations between how close two areas are spatially, and how similar the two represented objects are - for instance, the concept of dogs is often found to be near the subject's concept of wolves - there are also cases in which adjacent concepts represent what seem to us to be two very different things or properties.

We examine a speaker of English until we satisfy ourselves that we have found the location of his concept of rabbits. We stimulate it, and he says "rabbits," and "you must have hit my rabbit concept, my mind is filled with different images of rabbits." The scientists then probe a nearby area, and the rabbit concept also becomes active, but two other concepts at other places in the conceptual area of the brain also become active. The subject says, "undetached rabbit part, yes, now I'm thinking about a rabbit's leg, but still attached to his body." We stimulate one of the other two concept areas directly, and the subject says "detach, I'm getting all kinds of images of things detaching: bumpers falling off cars, airline tickets being detached from receipt stubs, and so on." We stimulate the other area and the subject says "parts, parts of things, parts of bodies, parts of machines, parts of houses." The concept of an undetached rabbit part is a complex concept in that it includes other concepts, such as the concepts of detachment, parts, and negation, compared to the concept of rabbits. There is, similarly, a difference in the brain, the future scientists argue, between imagining a rabbit, and imagining an undetached rabbit part. When you imagine an undetached rabbit part you mentally focus, as it were, on the part.

We then apply what we have learned as we examine the brain of the native as he spots a rabbit and cries "Gavagai." We determine whether the concepts active in his brain have the general configuration of the concept active in the brain of the English speaker as he said "rabbit," or of the configuration active when he said, "undetached rabbit part."

To say, as a mind-body dualist might, that there is no physical difference between the two events of imagining is to deny materialism of the minimal supervenience variety. According to this type of materialism, the mental supervenes on the physical, which means that any change in the mental is also a change in the physical, but not vice versa. When we go from imagining a rabbit to imagining one of its undetached parts, this is a change in the mental, which is either in itself a physical change (if we, as Searle does, simply assume that mental events are a type of physical event, see Chapter 3), or underlain in some way by a physical change.

One sort of response to this is to say that we are merely inferring which concept is active, but the speaker himself knows directly. Worse, though, one might object that this inference process is subject to exactly the same problems that the original process of determining reference using only external factors was: We are attempting to map some things (either word tokens, externally, or "concept" tokens, internally) onto real world referents. There is a difference however. Which thing a word refers to depends on something else, which concept it is associated with. What a concept is of, or represents, on the other hand is best thought of as a matter of what thing that concept is causally related to (including other concepts). These causal relations are all traceable from the third-person point of view.

To deny this will ultimately amount to a denial of supervenience, in the same way that supervenience is denied in the case of mental images. Kripke, for instance offers an objection to materialism which runs as follows: It seems possible that a future science could tell a subject he was in pain, based on its theory of which sorts of brain states constitute pains, and yet the subject not be in pain.[20] The response to this is that when we really have the correct theory of pain, however, counterexamples such as the one Kripke imagines will not happen. It merely seems to us that we can imagine cases in which the relevant brain state exists yet the subject is not in pain. For a long time people have thought they could imagine perpetual motion, yet it violates laws of physics, and hence is not possible. By analogy, when we really have the correct theory of how to individuate a person's concepts, there will be no indeterminacy about what the words associated with those concepts refer to.

Perhaps one reason why Searle does not not consider the possibility of removing the indeterminacy from the third-person point of view is that he accepts Kripke's idea that the first-person point of view is not reducible to the third-person point of view.[21] This irreducibility seems to leave open the possibility that what is needed to remove the indeterminacy is part of the irreducible component of the first-person point of view. In the next Chapter, we will examine Searle's views about the ontology of the mental in more detail.

Endnotes

[1] See Chapter 7 of *Intentionality*.

[2] "Contemporary Philosophy in the United States," in *The Blackwell Companion to Philosophy*, eds. Nicholas Bunnin and E.P. Tsui-James, Oxford: Blackwell Publishers Ltd., 1996, p. 8.

[3] See Austin's books *How To Do Things With Words*, Oxford: Oxford University Press, 1962; *Philosophical Papers*, Oxford: Oxford University Press, 1961; and *Sense and Sensibilia*, Oxford: Oxford University Press, 1962.

[4] *Mind, Language, and Society*, p. 141.

[5] See Putnam's 1962 article, "It Ain't Necessarily So," *The Journal of Philosophy*, **59**, pp. 658-671.

[6] See Kripke's book *Naming and Necessity*, Cambridge, Mass.: Harvard University Press, 1972. See also Keith Donnellan's article "Speaking of Nothing," *The Philosophical Review*, **83**, pp. 3-32.

[7] See Frege's "On Sense and Nominatum," 1892, reprinted in *The Philosophy of Language*, ed. A.P. Martinich, Oxford: Oxford University Press, 1990.

[8] *The Rediscovery of the Mind*, p. 157.

[9] *Speech Acts*, p. 90.

[10] See *Naming and Necessity*, p. 97. See also pp. 235-236 of *Intentionality*.

[11] See, for example, pp. 244-246 of *Intentionality*.

[12] See *Intentionality*, p. 255.

[13] This argument comes from Keith Donnellan, "Proper Names and Identifying Descriptions," *Synthese*, **21** (1970), pp. 335-358.

[14] "Indeterminacy, Empiricism, and the First Person," *The Journal of Philosophy*, **LXXXIV**, No. 3, pp. 123-147.

[15] This review appears in *The Structure of Language*, eds. Jerry Fodor and Jerrold Katz, Englewood Cliffs, NJ: Prentice-Hall, 1964, pp. 547-578.

[16] "Indeterminacy, Empiricism, and the First Person," p. 124.

[17] *Ibid.*, p. 144.

[18] New York: MacMillan Publishing Co. Inc., 1958.

[19] *Ibid.*, para. 243.

[20] See Kripke's *Naming and Necessity*, Cambridge, Mass.: Harvard University Press, 1972.

[21] See, for example, pp. 116-117 of *The Rediscovery of the Mind*.

3
Mind

I believe it is a profound mistake to try to describe and explain mental phenomena without reference to consciousness.

"Consciousness, Unconsciousness, and Intentionality," 1989

Introduction

The behaviorists sought to explain mental phenomena in terms of dispositions to respond to stimuli, and saw no need to even mention consciousness, much less provide a theory of it. But by the late 1970s, when Searle's interests were shifting from the philosophy of language to the philosophy of mind, the influence of behaviorism was rapidly shrinking. One of its replacements, though, artificial intelligence, also saw no need to address the subject of consciousness, and it was at this theory that Searle directed his criticisms. A particular branch of artificial intelligence, which Searle called "Strong AI," contained the working assumption that if a computer program could duplicate the output of the human mind, that computer program would be able to endow any computer that ran it with intentional mental states. This implies, for instance, that a computer program which can allow a computer to give the same answers to questions that a person would give has endowed that computer with the ability to *understand* language. This assumption, however, is behavioristic: Only input and output matter, not what's going on inside. In response to Strong AI, Searle devised an ingenious argument which seemed to show both that there are definite requirements on what sorts of internal processes produce the output, and that computers do not have the correct sort of internal processes to produce mental states. And, while Searle's argument was not originally framed in terms of the need for *consciousness*, it soon became apparent that one such internal process which might be required for the having of intentional states is consciousness. Before one can be said to understand a language, for instance, one must be *aware* of what the words of that language mean.

The realization that the ability to have intentional states might require consciousness motivated a deeper look into the question of what consciousness is. At the time, however, very few philosophers or psychologists were thinking about consciousness. One reason for this of course was the hegemony of behaviorism, but there were others, including one Searle saw as a kind of fear of the intractable:

> I think there are many deep reasons for this fear of consciousness in contemporary analytic philosophy. One of the most important of these is that the presuppositions and methods of contemporary philosophy are ill-equipped to deal with the subjectivity of conscious states.[1]

One reason why philosophy was not equipped to deal with consciousness (especially considered from the subjective, or first-person point of view) was that philosophers were stuck in a false dichotomy: Either materialism or dualism must be true. But materialism, the view that mental states are identical to physical states of the brain, could not explain why mental states seem to be different from all other physical states. The other position, dualism, the view the mental states are non-physical, had failed to elaborate on the nature of these non-physical things or properties. Materialism couldn't say what was special about mental states, while dualism couldn't say anything about them at all. Into this dilemma Searle stepped with a third possibility, one which explains what is special about mental states, while acknowledging their physicality. First we will examine Searle's attack on Strong AI, then we will turn to his work on the nature of mental states and consciousness.

The Chinese Room

Perhaps the piece of philosophy for which Searle is best known is something called the Chinese room argument.[2] During the 1970s, researchers in artificial intelligence began to claim that their computer programs endowed computers with intentional states. At Yale, computer scientist Roger Schank had developed a program which could take a short story as input, and then provide answers to questions about the story. This rather nice program would have gone largely unnoticed in the philosophical community except for one fact: Schank claimed that the programmed computer's ability to provide the answers showed that it *understood* the story.

One of the things which disturbed Searle about such claims was that he felt they were due in part to a residual behaviorism which the artificial intelligence community had inherited from psychologists and philosophers. On a behaviorist conception of a mental state such as understanding, all that is required for understanding is correct behavior. What happens in the mind is nothing more than an inchoate play of images and thoughts, and has little to do with the question of what understanding is. This movement in artificial intelligence had a parallel movement in philosophy, known as Turing machine functionalism,[3] which was rapidly attracting those philosophers who were fleeing the sinking ship of behaviorism. Coupled with the new and powerful theory of functionalism, the claims of computers having intentional states were much more than just loose talk on the part of some AI researchers. They were part of a large new paradigm for understanding the mind: the computer metaphor.

The distinction between the physical computing machine - made these days out of silicon, plastic and steel - and its abstract program, is crucial to this debate. The debate centers around the abstract program, not the physical computing machine. Searle's position is that merely running a certain program can never guarantee that intentional states will be produced. More exactly, in this case Searle is arguing that running a program is never logically sufficient to produce understanding.

If we suppose that Schank's programmed computer is able to answer any question put to it, the problem for Searle was that of somehow getting inside the computer to show that in spite of its correct behavior, it lacks true understanding. It is an important fact about computers and computer programs that virtually any physical computing machine can run (or *instantiate*) any computer program. Just about any physical object can be used as a computer, including collections of beer cans, water pipes, or the silicon-based computers we prefer today. Also, however, a human being can be a computer, and it was this possibility which gave Searle what he wanted: In order to know for certain whether the computer is actually understanding, *we can be the computer.* Note in what follows that much of Searle's argumentative force depends on our taking the point of view of the person in the room, on seeing the situation from the first-person point of view.

Searle envisaged a scenario in which he is in a room with a large computer program written to allow whatever runs it to understand the Chinese language. Outside the room expert Chinese speakers write questions in Chinese characters on slips of paper and insert them through a slot in the door. Searle takes the questions and writes out an answer by following his program, which has sentences in it such as: "If the first character is ☐ and the second character is ☐ then write ☐," and so on. Outside the room the experts agree that whatever is inside the room understands Chinese, based on the fact that the answers are uniformly correct and appropriate. It seems quite clear, however, that Searle has no understanding of Chinese, based on the apparent fact that he has no idea what any of the characters mean, and hence has no idea what he is referring to when he writes them down. It seems equally clear that a standard computer in the same situation is doing exactly what Searle is doing, simply matching character forms and spitting out whatever is contained in its program's "write" statements.

Searle prefers to present the Chinese room argument in terms of syntax and semantics: Computers have syntax for the "symbols" they manipulate, but they lack semantic knowledge about them, that is, they do not know what they mean. The problem with posing the dispute in terms of syntax and semantics is that the meanings of those unfamiliar terms then needs to be looked into, and this makes the debate much more complex and much less intuitive. Another problem with putting the argument in terms of syntax is that Searle has also argued that the computer is not even performing *syntactical* operations. Speaking strictly, computers do not even manipulate *ones* and *zeroes* intrinsically, since interpreting a certain voltage level in a certain part of the computer as a 1 and another voltage level as a 0 is an intentional act which we must perform in understanding what the computer does. More simply, then, without employing the syntax/semantics distinction, the debate comes down to the conflict between these two claims:

Schank: Everything that runs the program understands.

Searle: I run the program and do not understand.

The computationalists cannot abandon their liberal approach in letting just about anything be a computer without abandoning one of their key premises: The program contains everything needed to produce mental states. The argument comes down to the truth or falsity of Searle's claim that he does not understand Chinese.

Responses to the Chinese Room

The adherents of the idea that mentality is captured by computer programs face the task of refuting what appears to be a devastating yet unassailable argument in order to justify their entire research program.

Many of their initial replies were published along with Searle's responses to them in the original Chinese room article. We will review some of the stronger replies which have emerged, and discuss how Searle either has or might respond to them.

The Systems Reply

Of all the attempts to reply mounted by the artificial intelligence community, the most popular is what Searle calls "the systems reply." It runs as follows: Perhaps Searle is correct in claiming that he does not understand Chinese, but he is only part of a larger system, made up of Searle, the program and the room together. This larger system does understand Chinese because it can answer correctly. The fact that Searle, a part of the system, does not understand Chinese is no more damaging to the claim that the system understands Chinese than the claim that your pituitary gland doesn't understand English is to the claim that you understand English. There is no reason to think that each of a system's parts has all of the properties which the system as a whole possesses.

Searle's response to this is that he can again become the entire system by memorizing the program. Then he is free to leave the room and sit in person with the experts, writing out replies to their questions. He may accidentally begin to learn what some of the symbols mean; for instance someone might hold up an apple when writing a symbol. Accidental cases like this merely serve to bolster Searle's claim, though: This learning is due to Searle's own intrinsic mental intentionality, not to the program.

The Access Reply

A second, related line of response which the computationalists can give at this point is to argue that we are not always aware of everything which we can do or understand. The idea that being the computer allows us to see what is going on inside it depends on a further claim that the workings of our minds are transparent to us.

Suppose a friend is trying to teach you differential equations, a subject you believe you are horrible at. The friend writes out a problem and asks you to write down the answer. You stare at the symbols, thinking that it may as well be Chinese writing for all you know, since you have no idea what they mean or what the answer might be. "I give up," you say to your friend. "Look," he urges, "just write down what you think the answer is." "All right," you reply, "but I have no idea what I'm doing." You stare at the symbols, then write out a couple of numbers and symbols as an answer. "That's right," your friend exclaims, "Now try another one." Again you get the right answer, and again and again. The verdict here seems to be that you do understand differential equations even though you do not know that you do and in fact believe that you do not.

This sort of situation is not as unlikely as it seems, as revealed by certain cases in which brain-damaged patients have capabilities which they swear they lack. These cases seem to establish at least the possibility that a person might have a certain intentional state without knowing that he has it. Certain patients with damage to the visual cortex exhibit a phenomenon which has come to be called blindsight. "Here is the paradox:" says neuropsychologist Lawrence Weiskrantz "human patients in whom the occipital lobe is damaged say that they are blind in that part of the visual field that maps onto the damaged V1." These patients retain certain visual abilities, apparently unconsciously.

> The first clue about residual vision in people with visual cortex damage came from a study at MIT in 1973 (Poppel, *et al*) in which brain damaged U.S. war veterans were asked simply to move their eyes to the positions of a brief spot of light shone into their blind fields. The position of the light was varied from trial to trial in a random order. As they could not 'see', the subjects thought the instruction odd, but it emerged that their eyes did, in fact, move to the correct position.... [4]

They are also able to indicate with an arm movement the direction of a beam of light moving along a screen in front of them. It is known that there are several routes by which visual information leaves the eyes, and current thinking is that one of these routes must be intact in blindsight patients. In other words, their brains can apparently see things without any of the sort of conscious activity that we sighted people associate with seeing. In *Intentionality*, Searle seems to allow that blindsight patients do have intentional states, but that "the Intentional content produced by their optical stimulation is not realized in the way that our...contents are realized."[5]

This raises several important questions, not the least of which is what consciousness itself is and to what degree, or whether if at all, it is necessary to the cognitive functioning of the human being. If we can respond to visual stimuli without consciousness, why do we need consciousness? Variations of this problem have become known as the zombie problem; a zombie is a hypothetical being who has the perceptual and cognitive capacities of a human being without possessing conscious.

Another question raised by the existence of blindsight concerns the concept of seeing in general. Is it correct to describe what the blindsight patients are able to do as seeing? If consciousness is a necessary condition for the attribution of mental states, this opens up many other questions about why this is so. Why do we insist that something be conscious before it can have mental states? Later, Searle proposed something called the connection principle, which explains the connection intentional states have to consciousness. According to that idea, what the blindsight person gains is an intentional state, because the states involved are potentially conscious states in a normal brain. In the case of blindsight, there is simply a pathological "blockage" which prevents the state from being conscious.[6]

A variation of this reply might be called the multiple personality response, or MPD response. People with MPD often seem to have intentional states in one personality which they lack in another personality. One personality might have a strong desire to smoke, for instance, which another one lacks completely. Similarly, *remembering that* is an intentional state type, with a definite intentional content. People with MPD notoriously have autobiographical memories which are segregated according to personality. One personality only has memories from the times when it was "dominant," or "in charge." Perhaps, then, the reply goes, Searle at some level, in some way, does understand Chinese, even though he spends a lot of time denying that he does. The primary problem with the MPD reply, though, is that it stretches our ordinary, folk psychological concepts of the mental to a breaking point. Hence it is not clear how relevant this very strange phenomenon is to our normal intentionality.

The Speed Reply

A second line of response to the Chinese room story points to the extreme lengths of time it would actually take a person to follow such a program.[7] Perhaps the speed with which computers follow programs is a factor in allowing programs to endow computers with intentionality, these respondents argue. Sometimes the speed at which something moves is the crucial element in allowing it to perform a given function. Flapping your wings slowly doesn't produce flying, but flapping them really fast can do the trick. This reply deviates from the classical, more abstract approach to AI though, in which the programs are vital, while the particular speed at which they run is a peripheral issue.

This sort of reply might equally be taken to be a criticism of the willingness of the founders of computer science to let just about anything count as a computer. Certainly just about anything can be *used* a computer, but only certain things are *useful* as computers. This way of thinking seems to lead to unacceptable results when it is applied in other areas. For instance, consider the claim that, since anything can be used to represent something - I can use salt shaker to represent where my car was when it was hit by another car - virtually every object on earth is a representation. The remedy for this is just to point out that we only use certain things as representations because their properties match our properties in the right way. Some things are too big, or too small, for us to use as representations. Since the liberalism of letting anything play the role of (physical) computer is what allows Searle to pose his argument, one possible line of approach for his opponents is to consider tightening up the criteria for what can be a computer.

The response to the speed reply must be that we need some independent reason why speed matters. Speed doesn't seem to affect whether we believe that a computer is adding, for instance. We just allow that some computers add much faster than others. One way, additionally, Searle might argue that speed is irrelevant whereas consciousness is would be to point out that as long as we suspect that the computer is not conscious, we will to an equal degree suspect that the computer does not have intentional states. Obviously this points to a connection between consciousness and intentionality, one which Searle began to pursue after the furor over the Chinese room had died down.

Diagnosis

Searle regards the Chinese room argument as a refutation of Strong AI, or Turing machine functionalism. It is an argument from the first-person perspective in the same way that Searle's response to Quine is. Together the arguments point to a pattern, a vein which Searle has tapped: the behaviorist and computationalist theories of mind are vulnerable to attack from this direction, from the first-person point of view. As usual, after the arguments comes the treatment for the refuted. Searle's diagnosis is that there is a residual behaviorism in this branch of artificial intelligence, in that the task they set themselves is that of programming a computer to match the input-output patterns of humans; what goes on in between has at the start been ruled out as irrelevant. The Chinese room thought experiment works as a sort of remedy for this tendency:

Once we see that it is both conceptually and empirically possible for a system to have human capacities in some realm without having any intentionality at all, we should be able to overcome this impulse.[8]

Searle also sees a residual dualism in Strong AI. Programs are independent of the physical machines which instantiate or run them and have the same sort of abstract quality that numbers or other mathematical entities have. You can destroy copies of Windows 98, but you cannot destroy Windows98, in the same way that you cannot destroy the number 5. Since the adherents of Strong AI consider the program to be independent of any of its physical realizations, and they consider the mind to be a computer program, they must consider the mind to be independent of its physical realization in the brain. Searle says that:

> The single most surprising discovery that I have made in discussing these issues is that many AI workers are quite shocked by my idea that actual human mental phenomena might be dependent on actual physical-chemical properties of actual human brains.[9]

An interesting aspect of such a dualism is that it hides the mind in what is typically considered to be a separate ontological category: the abstract. One might make a division into three intuitive ontological categories or three types of existing things: physical things like rocks and chairs, mental things such as thoughts and dreams, and abstract things such as numbers, mathematical equations, and computer programs. It may be that the materialist has succeeded in chasing the mind out of the category of the mental by simply eliminating that category (or in Searle's case, rejecting the idea that mental properties are by definition not physical properties, see below). Instead of scurrying into the physical category, however, the mind has escaped into the realm of the abstract. One approach the materialist might take is to attempt a reduction of the abstract to something physical, but this promises to be a very difficult task.

It is curious that the plausibility of there being a program such as the one Searle has in the room is also not questioned more frequently. The idea that there could be a program which would allow a person to converse in a natural language about any topic, amounts to saying that the entire human intellect is in some form algorithmic. The idea that there can be such a program also assumes that we can solve the *background problem*, the problem of getting all of our background knowledge and abilities into the computer.

There is another interesting curiosity about the argument, which also works to show some sort of a connection between intentionality and consciousness. If the computationalists are bold enough to claim that they have written a program, which produces consciousness when it is followed or instantiated, Searle's strategy will not work. In order to use his strategy, Searle would have to follow the program and realize that he is not conscious. But surely this is impossible. Indeed, the idea that you could realize that you are not conscious has in it as much falsity in it as Descartes' claim that you cannot doubt your own existence has truth.

This seems to be where the debate ends, at least for now: Barring the rather unlikely possibilities that something in Searle does understand Chinese, or that somehow he will understand Chinese if he simply moves faster, it seems that Searle is right that there is more to understanding than correct behavior. What then is needed before there is true understanding? The brain has certain causal powers which it possesses because of its evolutionary history and physiological makeup. One causal power which is vital, according to Searle, is consciousness.

Searle's emphasis on causal powers is one reason why a clear distinction must be kept between the physical computing machines, and the program. The problem with using the physical sense of "computer" is that such machines may have all sorts of causal powers we do not know about. One causal power which physical computing machines must possess at a bare minimum is the power to move their program counter - which we might think of as a little arrow which points to the part of the program which is now executing. Can we be completely certain that the causal power to move the program counter is not also the causal powers to produce consciousness? One must admit that this is a very remote possibility, but still a logical possibility.

An Aristotelian Compromise

What we may have here is a modern version of a problem which Aristotle was aware of, and formulated a response to: the things we know about seem to be composites of both form and matter. Searle is insisting that the matter (or at least the particular physical realization of the computer) is important, while the computationalists are insisting that only the form is important. Everything that exists is a composite of both form and matter, though, according to Aristotle. We understand the human body, for instance, in terms of levels of form/matter structures. Each of the different organ systems contains physical objects, the heart, the lungs, etc. engaged in certain functional interactions. Each of these objects is then analyzed in the same way. It is made up of tissues engaged in functional interactions, these tissues consist of interacting cells, the cells consist of interacting organelles, which consist of interacting molecules, which consist of interacting atoms, which consist of interacting subatomic particles, as far as we can go.[10]

The disagreement may be more about what level of the form/matter hierarchy is the right one to explain mental phenomena. If we are willing to go to a low enough level, all sides will agree that we have captured the relevant phenomena. For instance, we might model the molecular structure of an entire human body in a computer program. This program contains all the information needed to duplicate a human being's entire, functioning body. We might imagine that we employ this technique to move people great distances: A person steps into an "analyzer" which records all the relevant information about her constituent atoms. Then this information is transmitted to a base on the moon, where it is used by a "constructor" to rebuild the person, using as raw materials stockpiles of all the needed types of matter: carbon, hydrogen, iron, and so on. Since we captured all of this person's properties in the formal description of her that was sent to the moon, in so doing we captured all of her mental properties formally as well. Of course, this is not the sort of thing the computationalists had in mind, so it is not necessarily a vindication of their position. What it shows, however, is that the dispute is not fruitfully thought of a being between formal conceptions of mental states held by the computationalists and physical/causal conceptions in the case of Searle.

Rather, the problem is that the computationalists have claimed that mental states are capturable at a formal level which Searle regards as too "high," as opposed to the "lower" molecular level, which is perhaps too low, too fine-grained. Consciousness itself exists at one of these functional levels, so perhaps programs which encode this level in addition to one or more other levels would be sufficient to produce a being with intentionality. The current debate among scientists about what approach to consciousness is correct is partly about which level is correct: subatomic, molecular, cellular, or higher-level properties.

Consciousness as a Biological Phenomenon

In his 1997 book *The Mystery of Consciousness*,[11] Searle reviews several biological and philosophical theories of consciousness. The recent appearance of several competing biological theories of consciousness (e.g., those of Crick and Edelman) lends credence to Searle's emphasis on consciousness and to the idea that the mind's consciousness and its intentionality should be treated as biological phenomena:

> Some philosophers are reluctant to admit the existence of consciousness because they fail to see that the *mental* state of consciousness is just an ordinary biological, that is physical, feature of the brain.[12]

Mental properties do not need to be 'reduced' to physical properties, they simply are a type of physical property. Instead of thinking that "mental" implies "non-physical," we should think of the mental as being a subtype of the physical.[13]

Unlike many philosophers, Searle has a good grasp of scientific advances in understanding the brain, and more importantly, has good empirical instincts. Now that philosophers are increasingly finding brain science relevant to their thinking, many of them nevertheless attempt to evaluate the probabilistic, intuitive reasoning of the scientist against the standards of necessary truth which they are accustomed to. Scientist's ears do not perk up when philosophers tell them that it is logically possible they are mistaken. On the other hand, Searle is a rare example of the ability to be at home discussing either *a priori*, logical issues or empirical, scientific questions.

The Structural Features of Consciousness

Consciousness comes in a finite set of modalities. Searle lists eight compared to the usual five: sight, hearing, smell, touch, taste, the sense of balance, sensation of the body ("proprioception" or "somatosensation"), and "the stream of thought."[14] Another feature within each modality is a pleasant-unpleasant dimension. Smells, for instance, can be pleasant or unpleasant, and this turns out to be true of each of the modalities, with the type of pleasantness or unpleasantness being specific to the modality: "pleasant smells are not pleasant in the way the pleasant thoughts are pleasant."[15] Consciousness is unified, in the sense that the different modalities blend into a single conscious state. One way to see the relentless unifying tendency of consciousness is via something called the ventriloquism effect: If you see someone talking and hear words which fit the lip movements of the person, you will tend to hear the sounds *as* coming from the person's lips, even if the sound is actually coming from a speaker behind you. Consciousness is also unified in the temporal dimension; conscious experiences are organized over short stretches of time, by something such as short-term memory.

Conscious states are usually directed at things outside of themselves:

> Most, but not all, consciousness is intentional. I may, for example, simply be in a mood of depression or elation without being depressed or elated about anything in particular. In these cases, my mood, as such, is not intentional.[16]

Conscious states also have subjectivity, in that there is something it is like to have them. When you wonder what it would be like to be shot, you are wondering what the subjective features of that experience are, in the same way you might wonder what it would be like to be a dolphin.

Our conscious states come to us with a structure. This is easiest to see in the case of vision. When we look at something, we do not see it as an undifferentiated mass of colors and edges. Rather, what we see is structured for us by our background perceptual capacities into definite objects, with definite properties. Perhaps the primary rule of structure is that what we see is organized into a figure and a background, as the Gestalt psychologists pointed out. When we visually focus on something, we see it against a background, and items in the background can in turn be focused on, causing the item previously focused on to recede into the background. Another feature of conscious states is the aspect of familiarity. This aspect comes in degrees, ranging from very familiar people, such as one's parents, to cases in which everything seems unfamiliar such as those cases where we are unable to categorize anything at all, an effect certain painters strive for in their work. Searle is clear that the aspect of familiarity is not a feeling which is separable from the rest of the visual experience of a familiar thing:

> When I see my shoes, for example, I do not have both a visual experience of the shoes, and a feeling of familiarity, but rather I *see* the shoes *as* shoes and *as* mine.[17]

It is not clear that this is correct, however. One might argue that cases of *déjà vu* are cases where we experience the feeling of familiarity without the recognition. Epileptic seizures are also famous for producing feelings of familiarity without recognition.[18] When we see a familiar object, however, it may be true that we cannot draw a separation between the act of recognition and the feeling of familiarity *from the first-person point of view*. Since Searle believes that the ontology of the conscious state is a first-person ontology (i.e., that it is ontologically subjective), his thinking may be that if a distinction cannot be drawn from the first-person point of view, there is no distinction there. Searle's views on the ontology of the mental are our next topic.

The Ontology and Epistemology of the Mental

Dualism continued its slow decline during the 20th Century, due partly to the longstanding inability of dualists to say what exactly the mind or mental properties are, or how they causally interact with the brain and its physical properties, but partly also to a new threat. The idea that a physical thing could not possibly produce what minds produce began to be reconsidered, both as the brain was discovered to be much more complex than had been imagined, and as physical computing devices began to achieve what had previously been achievable only by minds, such as mathematical calculations. Materialism was not quite ready yet to take dualism's place, however. The primary stumbling block to getting a materialist theory of the mind is that our conscious mental states are different from any physical states we know of. The following argument looks rather robust:

The Objectivity Argument

Any physical process can be observed by more than one person.

Conscious events occurring in one person's brain cannot be observed by any other person.

Therefore, conscious events are not physical processes.

Even if we allow that consciousness is somehow produced by the brain, the brain seems to have two types of properties:

Objective properties of a set of neurons include their electrical charges, their size, their weight, their chemical composition, their glucose utilization, and so on.

Subjective properties of a set of neurons are the conscious properties of those neurons.

I can certainly observe the objective properties of the neurons making up your brain, but there is simply no way for me to observe the subjective properties, it would seem.

Two very different positions can still be derived from the distinction between objective and subjective properties, however. In accord with the objectivity argument, a property dualist believes that the objective properties of your brain states are physical, while the subjective properties are non-physical, solely mental, properties. Searle, contrary to this, holds that both the objective and the subjective properties are physical properties - mental properties are a type of physical property. Searle's diagnosis of the objectivity argument is that the first premise is false: There in fact *are* physical properties and processes which only one person can ever know about.

It is important to get a better fix on how Searle is using the word "subjective" when he talks about the subjectivity of conscious states. He describes two ways to interpret the subjective/objective distinction, an epistemic way, and an ontological way. On the epistemic interpretation of the distinction, the terms "subjective" and "objective" function primarily as qualities of judgments. Judgements are subjective because they depend on feelings and attitudes and on the point of view one is taking. Objective judgements are made true or false not by people's feelings, but by the facts of the world. On the ontological interpretation, "subjective" and "objective" refer to modes of existence:

> In the ontological sense, pains are subjective entities, because their mode of existence depends on being felt by subjects. But mountains, for example, in contrast to pains, are ontologically objective because their mode of existence is independent of any perceiver or mental state.[19]

Ontologically subjective facts can still be epistemically objective, because, for instance, the fact that you feel a pain in your right leg is not a fact which is made true by anyone's opinions, attitudes, or feelings.

Introspection is Not Like Perception

We speak about introspection as if it were a sort of internal seeing. Normal seeing, however, includes both an object of perception, and a perceiver, engaged in perceiving. Theories of introspection which model it on perception are mistaken, according to Searle:

> Where conscious subjectivity is concerned, there is no distinction between the observer and the thing observed, between the perception and the object perceived. The model of vision works on the presupposition that there is a distinction between the thing seen and the seeing of it. But for "introspection" there is simply no way to make this separation. Any introspection I have of my own conscious state is itself that conscious state.[20]

Conscious states are the only states of which Berkeley's dictum, "to be is to be perceived" is true, on Searle's account. This would require a distinction between the conscious state and our introspection of it, and "we cannot make this distinction for conscious states."[21] Ontologically subjective properties of the brain are capable of containing their own awareness, on this conception, and in this respect they are quite different from the other physical properties.

Relational vs. Intrinsic Theories of Awareness

This seems a lot to ask of a single conscious state, however. On Searle's account a conscious state such as a feeling of pain must have the following four features:

1) It must have an intentional content.

2) It must be conscious.

3) It must contain its own awareness.

4) The conscious properties of the state must be able to cause and guide behavior (especially behavior directed at what the intentional content represents).

The question of the relation between the ontology of conscious states and our knowledge of them is perhaps the most vexing problem we know of. In order to get a better fix on Searle's views both on consciousness and on intentionality we need to contrast Searle's approach with another theory which differs at crucial points. On Searle's theory, our awareness of the subjective properties (i.e., the conscious aspectual shapes) of a conscious state is *intrinsic* to that state, but what might a non-intrinsic, or *relational* theory of awareness look like? On such a theory, a separation can be made between conscious states and our knowledge or awareness of them - they can *be* without being perceived. Hence, a relational theory allows, as strange as it sounds, conscious states which the subject has no knowledge of.

Knowledge is a Two-Part Relation

One way to grasp the difference between intrinsic and relational theories of awareness is to look at their differing descriptions of what is going on at the edges of consciousness. Consider the following, from Searle's discussion in *The Rediscovery of the Mind* about the center-periphery structure of conscious states:

> We are conscious of a very large number of things that we are not attending to or focusing our attention upon. For example, up to this moment I have been focusing my attention on the philosophical problem of describing consciousness, and I have not been paying any attention to the feeling of the chair against my back, the tightness of my shoes, or the slight headache I have from drinking too much wine last night. Nonetheless, all of these phenomena are part of my conscious awareness.[22]

Is it right, however, to say that he is aware of, or conscious of, the tightness of his shoes, for example? Clearly he is not attending to the tightness, but is it right to say that he is aware of it? Here, the relational theorist will argue, is an example of (at least a part of) a conscious state which the subject is not aware of. When Searle becomes aware of the tightness, what happens, on the relational account, is that some other brain process causally connects with the part of the brain responsible for the feeling of tightness.

Knowledge is always at least a two-part relation between a knower and what she knows, the relational theorist would argue. What is required for knowledge is a certain two-part functional structure. Without this structure, there can be no knowledge about anything, including conscious states, *even if there are conscious states present*. There is, on the relational view, a distinction between having a conscious state, and knowing about one's conscious state. Knowledge about conscious states requires a conscious state, plus, one suspects, processes which do something with the conscious state, such as using them to guide activity. Notice, in the example above, when Searle truly does become aware of the tightness, now it is open to him to do something about it, such as taking his shoes off. Knowledge is a relational or complex property of a set of entities (knower, object), whereas consciousness is an intrinsic or simple property of a neuronal ensemble, on this alternative conception. We might call conscious states which the subject lacks awareness of states of *bare consciousness*.

Consciousness itself is not sufficient for knowledge on the relational theory. Rather, states of bare consciousness must enter into causal contact with another brain state, and these larger conscious states are those in which the subject is aware of his conscious state. It is perhaps the existence of this brain process which contacts conscious states and produces an awareness of them which leads to the tendency in everyday talk to lapse into a perceptual model of introspection: The bare conscious state is like the object of perception, and the other process is like a perceiver. Notice that the two positions need not disagree about Searle's claim that "any introspection I have of my own conscious state is itself that conscious state."[23] On the relational account, the more complex state in which the subject is aware of something can still include both the object-like state and the perceiver-like state as part of a single, complex, conscious state.

The Homunculus Fallacy

In the discussion of relational theories of consciousness, the reader may have noticed that a dangerous fallacy lurks nearby. If there really were a perceiver in the brain, then we really have not explained consciousness, since we consider perception itself to be a conscious mental state. We would have a homunculus (Latin for "little man") inside the head; and now there is a conscious state inside this inner perceiver.[24] A dreaded infinite regress looms, and if that happens, we really have not explained consciousness at all. Searle accepts this sort of criticism.[25]

It may be an error to assume that a relational theory of conscious awareness requires a homunculus, however. Relational theories require *something like* a perceiver, but there does not seem to be anything which requires that this perceiver have all the abilities of a full human mind. For instance, the state which stands in for the perceiver in a relational theory could simply be another brain process which is using the bare conscious state as its input. The homunculus objection commits the fallacy of false analogy: it misinterprets the analogy between perception and introspection, in the same way that one would misunderstand Bohr's analogy between the atom and the solar system if one were to look for a self-luminous star at the center of an atom. The regress can be halted by understanding the analogy correctly. All a relational theory of conscious awareness requires is two things or processes, one being something like an object of perception, the other being something like a perceiver - not something identical to a perceiver.

On Searle's view all conscious states contain their own awareness. Since being aware of something is a type of intentional state, this implies that all conscious states are intentional states (non-intentional *features* of consciousness, such as the feeling of depression, are not conscious *states*). Ontological subjectivity is a primitive feature of conscious states that cannot be analyzed into separate ontological and epistemic components, on Searle's view. Ontologically subjective properties cannot be analyzed into ontologically objective properties. The relational conception, however, analyzes conscious states, and conscious intentional states into the same sorts of things and properties which everything else is made up of, and hence does not require a separate ontological category.

Knowledge of Other's Conscious States

Relational accounts of conscious awareness also open up the possibility of one person knowing about another person's bare conscious states, in the same way in which the person herself knows about them. Since the relational theory has two components, something like a perceiver, and something like a perceptual object, these two components could be located in two different people.

Qualia are the conscious, subjective, properties of brain states, i.e., on Searle's theory, qualia are ontologically subjective. When I form a mental image of a green square, for instance, that image has two properties, or qualia: greenness and squareness. Consider the following thought experiment: Two subjects, call them the *bearer* of qualia, and the *sharer* of the bearer's qualia, could be hooked up, brain to brain, with something like a cable that carried electrical impulses from the bearer's brain into the sharer's brain.[26] One might call this a *qualia cable* since it would have the effect of enabling the sharer to experience the bearer's (bare) perceptual qualia "from the inside," for the period of time that they were connected. This possibility allows a way of conceiving of the qualities of subjective experience, or qualia, as *not* essentially private. Thus this approach would reject the second premise in the objectivity argument against materialism, as opposed to Searle, who rejects the first premise:

The Objectivity Argument

Any physical process can be observed by more than one person.

Conscious events occurring in one person's brain cannot be observed by any other person.

Therefore, conscious events are not physical processes.

A qualia cable is quite literally a possibility on a relational account of consciousness. It might be employed, for instance, between two patients prepared for neurosurgery, or between a patient and an adventurous cognitive scientist. As a way of testing the qualia cable in its early stages of development, the sharer can be asked to introspect and report what he is experiencing, which then can be compared with the bearer's reports. One obvious objection to the possibility of such a cable has to do with whether the sharer can be certain he is receiving a faithful copy of the bearer's qualia. It is important to notice, though, that the observer is in contact with the bearer's bare conscious states themselves, and not a copy of them. The qualia cable transmits not copies of the qualia, but the neural signals needed for the brains of the bearer and sharer to enter into a single, unified conscious state. The brain of the sharer contains a conscious state which is *bound* with part of the conscious state of the bearer. "Binding" is a technical term for some as yet unidentified brain process that knits together different areas of the brain into a unified conscious state, for instance areas of the brain representing shapes of objects and areas representing their colors - we see them together as colored shapes.[27] Most theories of binding posit electrical oscillations which synchronize activity of different cortical areas through phase locking, for instance at a frequency of 40 Hertz. If binding can occur across areas in one brain, why not across areas in two brains? The qualia cable allows the sharer to experience, or speaking loosely, to "perceive," the bearer's qualia.

Let us return to the four properties which Searle's theory attaches to conscious states and determine how those properties might be distributed on a relational approach. The four properties of conscious states are:

1) It must have an intentional content.

2) It must be conscious.

3) It must contain its own awareness.

4) The conscious properties of the state must be able to cause and guide behavior

The job of making a state conscious, the second property, might be achieved by a simple process such as synchronized oscillations. The third and fourth properties might be achieved not by the conscious state alone, but by its entering into the appropriate relation with the other, perceiver-like, state. The third and fourth properties are relational properties of the bare conscious state and the perceiver-like state together (e.g., being married is a relational property of husband and wife together), not intrinsic properties of the bare conscious state. The bare state itself is largely ineffective causally until it enters into the proper relation with the perceiver-like state, so that the original state is only intentional by virtue of its ability to relate to the other state (more on this below). What made the problem of explaining the ontology of conscious states seem either to be unsolvable or to require a separate ontological category was perhaps the insistence that one state must be found with all of these features.

This idea seems to explain certain criticisms which Searle makes of biological theories of consciousness. He wants a single process which accomplishes all four of the criteria above, and finds that the biologists offer no such thing. Perhaps the biologists are offering accounts of bare consciousness, not accounts of conscious awareness. Bare consciousness might be something like synchronized firing of neurons. A more complete biological theory of conscious awareness would include an account of bare consciousness, plus an account of the perceiver-like process.[28]

It is interesting to note that a qualia cable seems to render the first-person/third-person distinction obsolete. Does the sharer have first-person or third-person point of view on the bearer's qualia? In one respect he has first-person knowledge. The problem is that the sharer is still a different person from the bearer, so that if "third-person knowledge" means "knowledge which others have of the subject's states" (and "first-person knowledge" is defined as "knowledge the subject has of his own states"), the sharer *also* has third-person knowledge of the bearer's states.

A Solution to the Mind-Body Problem

Mental states, according to Searle, are both *caused by and realized in* brain states.[29] This is initially puzzling - usually when x causes y, x and y are two different things, or events. Searle provides us with the perfect example, however:

> The liquidity of water is both caused by and realized in the molecular cohesion of H_2O molecules.

The liquidity of water - the way it flows, and beads up due to its surface tension - is caused by the weak molecular bond which exists between H_2O molecules. There is nothing more to liquidity than molecular cohesion, however.

There is nothing wrong with talking about one property of a thing causing another property of that same thing. We might say that the dark color of a car causes it to heat up on a sunny day, for instance - a color property causes a temperature property. Here is how Searle describes the relation between the two types of property involved:

> It is a characteristic of the progress of science that an expression that is originally defined in terms of surface features, features accessible to the senses, is subsequently defined in terms of the micro-structure that causes the surface features. Thus, to take the example of solidity, the table in front of me is solid in the ordinary sense that it is rigid, it resists pressure, it supports books, it is not easily penetrable by most other objects such as other tables, and so on. Such is the commonsense notion of solidity. And in a scientific vein one can define solidity as whatever micro-structure causes these gross observable features. So one can say either that solidity just is the lattice structure of the system of molecules and that solidity so defined causes, for example, resistance to touch and pressure.[30]

The problem with the notion of "features accessible to the senses," however, is that when this analogy is applied to introspection, it results in exactly what Searle does not want: A perceptual theory of introspection. A second problem with this approach is that what Searle is referring to as the liquidity of water may be nothing more than the way water appears to us, that is, a secondary property of water. Secondary properties, on most accounts, involve both the perceiver and the object of perception - they arise out of the interaction between the two. The redness of an object is a secondary property on the classical conception, since it depends both on features of us (the responses of the cones in the retina, and the rest of the visual system) and on features of the object (its spectral reflectance capacities). This presumably is not the sort of direction Searle wants our discussion of the water example to go in, because it seems to be leading us toward a perceptual account of conscious states - they are a sort of secondary property that arises out of the interaction between something like a perceiver and something like a perceptual object.

If liquidity is not a secondary property, then it may be a relational property of some other type: it may be relational to an ontological level, or a level of description. Or it may simply be a relation to the distance we are from the water molecules, in the way that a group of blue and yellow dots looks green from a distance. Searle says that liquidity and cohesion are the same phenomenon at two "different levels of description of a substance."[31] That is the epistemology of the situation, but what about the ontology? The following now becomes a very important question: What is the metaphysical status of these levels? Are they ontological or epistemic? That is, are the levels in reality outside of us, or are they levels in our understanding of the phenomena?

Another question concerns how the macro-micro distinction is to be related to the mind-body problem. In the case of the mind/brain, what needs to be related are the first and the third-person points of view. But, how is this distinction to be reconciled with the macro-micro distinction, since the third-person view of the brain has both a micro level (recording from single neurons, for instance) and a macro level (brain processes such as face-recognition, which employ vast areas of the cortex).

The Connection Between Consciousness and Intentionality

What is the relation between the ability to be conscious and the ability to have intentional states? Do computers lack intentional states because they lack consciousness? Can beings who are not capable of consciousness still have intentional states? In 1989, in a paper entitled "Consciousness, Unconsciousness, and Intentionality,"[32] Searle outlined the nature of the connection between consciousness and intentionality. Searle's answer to the question of whether beings can have intentionality without consciousness is, No: Certain connections to consciousness are necessary for a mental state to have intentionality. According to Searle: "Only a being that could have conscious intentional states could have intentional states at all, and every unconscious intentional state is at least potentially conscious."[33] Searle refers to this claim as the *connection principal*.

Initially, unconscious intentional states, such as a belief which we are not currently consciously aware of, seem to separate consciousness from intentionality, since they retain their intentionality in spite of lacking consciousness. But they retain their intentionality, according to Searle, because they retain the potential to be objects of consciousness. Besides the desire to get clear on the role of consciousness in intentionality, another motive Searle had for arguing for the connection principal was that writers in the cognitive sciences were increasingly making use of the notion of unconscious rule following, or speaking of the human perceptual apparatus as making unconscious decisions. These ways of speaking might be taken to indicate that consciousness is not required for having intentional states, and they again threaten to open the door to letting computers have intentional states.

As we have seen, all intentional states have an aspectual character, and this character cannot be exhaustively or completely characterized solely in third-person terms, including neurophysiological terms, on Searle's view. In taking the first-person point of view on a conscious state, we are exposed to different causal features of the state than when we view it via third-person techniques. There is thus a strong connection between aspects and consciousness: To have an aspectual character is to bear some relation to consciousness, since consciousness is the medium so to speak in which the aspects exist. Intentional states must have aspects, and consciousness is required for the having of aspects, so intentional states require consciousness.

Unconscious intentional states have unconscious aspectual shapes. Unconscious aspectual shapes are like the magnetic traces on a computer diskette, which can be converted into words and pictures on the computer's monitor by other processes in the computer.[34] This analogy is of limited help, however, since both the magnetic traces and the state of the computer's monitor are unproblematically physical states. But when unconscious aspectual shape give rise to conscious aspectual shape, something rather miraculous happens, property instances of one ontological category give rise to property instances in another ontological category.

Aspectual Shape and Causal Relations

Another possibility, however, is that consciousness is simply the way in which the brains of humans and other animals achieve the function of representation, and that other ways to achieve intentionality and representation exist which do not require consciousness.

Consider another kind of aspect, called *causal aspects*. Any object exerts certain causal forces, and in turn is affected by causal forces coming from other objects. It is similarly important that any object also does *not* exert certain other causal forces and is *not* significantly affected by certain other causal forces of other objects. We want cookware, for instance, to not be affected by heat. Any two objects have aspects which are capable of causally interacting and aspects which are not. For instance, a photometer reacts to the light-emitting aspect of a glowing mass of plutonium, but does not causally react to its radiation, while a Geiger counter reacts to the radiation but not to the light.

The color aspect of a visual intentional state is capable of influencing behavior when I ask you to retrieve the red book from the shelf. On the other hand, the radiation emitted by the neurophysiological structures which realize that state is not causally capable of influencing the behavior we direct at the state's intentional object. Or at least the brain is not designed that way. One way to tell which properties of a physically realized representation are the causally important ones is to see which properties the system takes care to maintain. Some of the aspects under which two things interact are maintained and manipulated by the larger cognitive system which they are in. Consider a brain state which functions as a representation of Groucho Marx. The brain containing that state will take care to maintain the representationally important properties of that set of neurons, while it will neglect others. In the same way, we take care to maintain those properties of our external representations which are important for their representational function. The representationally important properties of books, for instance is the shape of the ink marks on the paper. We do not care about the temperature, weight, or smell of books, for instance, except insofar as they indicate the state of the truly important properties of the book, the ink marks. All representations are designed to be easy to use. In the case of books, it is important that there be a good contrast between the darkness of the ink and the lightness of the page, so that those who use the book as a representation can do so.

It may be correct that all intentionality presents its object in an aspectual character, but systems which do this may be only a specific form of a more general type of system: The aspects are those properties of the intentional state which are capable of playing a causal role in the production and execution of actions. Consciousness may be only the particular process which in the human brain is the way in which the aspectual shapes causally interact with the processes which execute behaviors. The special value which consciousness has for humans may be the way that it allows large, very detailed representations to causally interact, both among one another, and with action-producing (or inhibiting) processes, along many parallel lines at once. But, there may be other sorts of process that can allow for this. This line of thought can still accept the idea that the *primary function* of consciousness is to allow for intentionality, but without committing to the stronger claim that the process of consciousness is necessary for intentionality.

Intentionality and Intrinsicality

Anything can be used to represent anything else. For instance, I can use a salt shaker to represent where my car was when an accident occurred, and a bottle of ketchup to represent the other car. But it would be absurd to say that this means that everything on earth is a representation. Rather, something is a representation when someone uses it to stand for something else. Representation is a three-part relation between a represented (my car), a representation (the salt shaker) and a representer (me). It is thought that this sort of model of representation cannot work for mental representations, however, since we cannot have an internal representer - this would be a homunculus. What the relational theory of awareness suggests, however, is that this itself is a fallacy, there is no homunculus, but there is a brain process which stands in for the little man, which is the representer, the perceiver - like process above. Now, just as the external representer makes the representation stand for its object, does the perceiver-like brain process make the bare conscious state represent its object? This would imply that bare conscious states lack intentionality until they causally interact with the perceiver-like state.

There is some evidence that states of bare consciousness do in fact lack intentionality. Meditative states are a good example of states of bare consciousness. Consider the type of meditation where one listens one's breathing. What happens when one successfully enters into a meditative state is that one no longer hears the breathing sounds *as one's breathing*. Rather the meditator's consciousness contains only a bare conscious state. But notice that what happens at this moment is that the conscious state loses its intentionality. The qualia are no longer interpreted as the sound of breathing. In the lore of meditation, this is described as making "the self" go away. The relationalist would interpret this as meaning that the perceiver-like state has ceased functioning, and what is left in consciousness is just the bare conscious state. On a relational conception, bare conscious states must connect to the perceiver-like state in order to be intentional, in the same way that an object needs to connect with a representer in order to be a representation.

Endnotes

[1] See "Consciousness, Unconsciousness, and Intentionality," pp. 193-194.

[2] The original argument appears along with criticisms by others and Searle's replies in *The Behavioral and Brain Sciences*, **3** (1980), 417-457. A second series of criticisms was published along with Searle's replies in 1982: *The Behavioral and Brain Sciences*, **5**(1982), pp. 338-348.

[3] See Hilary Putnam's article "Minds and Machines," in *Dimensions of Mind*, ed. Sidney Hook, New York: New York University Press, 1960.

[4] See Lawrence Weiskrantz' recent book *Consciousness Lost and Found*, Oxford: Oxford Univ. Press, 1997. See also Poppel, *et al*, "Residual Visual Function After Brain Wounds Involving the Central Visual Pathway in Man," *Nature* (London), **243**, pp. 295-296.

[5] *Intentionality*, p. 47.

[6] See *The Rediscovery of the Mind*, p. 163.

[7] See Hofstader's, "Reductionism and Religion," *The Behavioral and Brain Sciences*, **3** (1980), 433-434. Patricia and Paul Churchland take a

similar position in "Could a Machine Think?," *Scientific American*, 1990, pp. 32-37.

[8] "Minds, Brains, and Programs," p. 423.

[9] *Ibid.*

[10] See W. G. Lycan's book *Consciousness*, Cambridge, Mass.: The M.I.T. Press, 1987, for a similar view.

[11] *The Mystery of Consciousness*, New York: The New York Review of Books, 1997.

[12] *The Rediscovery of the Mind*, p. 13.

[13] See *The Rediscovery of the Mind*, p. 14.

[14] *Ibid.*, p. 128.

[15] *Ibid.* p. 129.

[16] *Ibid.*, p. 130.

[17] *Ibid.*, p. 135.

[18] See Pierre Gloor's fascinating work: *The Temporal Lobe and the Limbic System*, Oxford: Oxford Univ. Press, 1997, pp. 701-702.

[19] *The Construction of Social Reality*, p. 8. See also *Mind, Language and Society*, pp. 44-45.

[20] *The Rediscovery of the Mind*, p. 97. See also *Mind, Language, and Society*, p. 72, and *The Rediscovery of the Mind*, pp. 143-144.

[21] *The Rediscovery of the Mind*, p. 144.

[22] *Ibid.*, pp. 137-138. Searle's main point here is to argue that the feeling of tightness in his shoes is not unconscious, as some might claim. The relational theorist agrees with Searle on this point, but disagrees with Searle's claim that we are aware of the tightness.

[23] *Ibid.*, p. 97.

[24] See Daniel Dennett, *Explaining Consciousness*, Boston: Little, Brown and Company, 1991, for an explication and criticism of the homunculus fallacy.

[25] See *The Rediscovery of the Mind*, pp. 212-214.

[26] This idea has been mentioned casually several times, but as far as I know, the first serious explicit proposal of it occurs in V. S. Ramachandran and William Hirstein, "Three Laws of Qualia: Clues From Neurology About the Biological Functions of Consciousness and Qualia," *The Journal of Consciousness Studies*, **4**, 1997, 429-57.

[27] See V.G. Hardcastle "Consciousness and the Neurobiology of Perceptual Binding," *Seminars in Neurology*, **17** (2), 1997, 163-170 for more information about theories of binding.

[28] V.S. Ramachandran and I offer such a theory in "Three Laws of Qualia," *op cit.*

[29] See Chapter 10 of *Intentionality*. See also *Minds, Brains and Science*, pp. 17-23.

[30] *Minds, Brains, and Science*, pp. 21-22.

[31] *Intentionality*, p. 168.

[32] Philosophical Topics, **XVII**, pp. 193-209. See also *Mind, Language, and Society*, pp. 86-89, and *The Rediscovery of the Mind*, pp. 155-164.

[33] *The Rediscovery of the Mind*, p. 132.

[34] *Mind, Language, and Society*, p. 87.

4
Reality

> *I regard the basic claim of external realism - that there exists a real world that is totally and absolutely independent of all of our representations, all of our thoughts, feelings, opinions, language, discourse, texts, and so on - as so obvious, and indeed as such an essential condition of rationality, and even of intelligibility, that I am somewhat embarrassed to have to raise the question and to discuss the various challenges to this view.*
>
> Mind, Language, and Society, 1998

Introduction

Research in the philosophies of mind and language increasingly has the other cognitive sciences such as neurobiology and cognitive linguistics to compare notes with and to keep it from disappearing into jargon or abstractions. In metaphysics, however, there remains the possibility of becoming unmoored from reality and common sense. To prevent this, metaphysics needs to re-anchor itself from time to time by returning to our everyday views about reality. Searle's attitude toward metaphysical issues reminds one of G.E. Moore's (1873-1958), one of the founders of analytic philosophy. In his authoritative book, *English Philosophy Since 1900*,[1] G.J. Warnock argues that Moore's *character* was decisive in ending the esoteric, uncommonsensical school of philosophy which preceded analytic philosophy - known as absolute idealism - as well as setting the tone for analytic philosophy to follow:

> He was not, and never had the least idea that he was, a much cleverer man than [his discussants] McTaggart, for example, or Bradley. It was in point of character that he was different, and importantly so. He seems to have been, in the first place, entirely without any of the motives that tend to make a metaphysician. He was neither discontented with nor puzzled by the ordinary beliefs of plain men and plain scientists.[2]

Figures such as Moore tend to appear in the history of philosophy when philosophy needs them. It took the simple-mindedness of a Socrates to question and to show the absurdity of the arcane theological theories about what pleased and displeased the gods which Greeks of his time followed. Similarly, it took Descartes' distrust of needless complexity to bring an end to the previous philosophical paradigm, based on impossibly complex modifications made by medieval thinkers to the already difficult Aristotle. Similarly, Searle's commensense mentalism provides the perfect counterpoint to behaviorism or computationalism in the philosophy of mind, and his commonsense realism provides the perfect balance for today's sophisticated relativisms. Ideally each of us has this commonsense character type within us, the sort inner voice which says at the right time in our thinking: "I'm lost. Let me return to what I'm certain of and start again."

Idealist philosophy in the 1890s, according to Warnock, had reached a state in which

> It was supposedly agreed on all hands that quite ordinary opinions were quite certainly defective; that common ways of speaking were almost always unsatisfactory....[3]

Moore's remedy for this is simply to point out that what is being denied is still more certain than its denial. In his article "Proof of an External World," he held up his two hands and proclaimed: "Here is one hand and here is another; therefore at least two things outside us exist." Or consider Moore's remark to the effect that, if time is unreal, does this mean that we don't have breakfast *before* lunch? Searle shares with Moore this delight in pointing out unintuitive consequences of his interlocutors' positions. Moore's challenge to the metaphysical skeptic - who denies we can have certainty about the world outside of our thoughts and perceptions - sometimes took the form of a list of claims which he was certain of, and willing to defend against skepticism, or relativism. Just as Moore's famous article "A Defense of Common Sense" begins with a list of truisms which he claims he knows to be true with certainty - such as that he has a body, that the earth existed for many years before he was born, and so on - Searle's *Mind, Language, and Reality* begins with a list of "default positions": There is a real world that exists independently of us, causation is a real relation, and so on.

Searle, at least his polemical side, also shares with Moore the ability to be motivated by what he perceives as wrongheadedness. Moore said:

> I do not think that the world or the sciences would ever have suggested to me any philosophical problems. What has suggested philosophical problems to me is things which other philosophers have said about the world or the sciences.[4]

Searle has this motivation, kindled by claims such as Schank's assertion that his computer program produced understanding, or Quine's claim that when people speak, what their words refer to is indeterminate. But Searle has another motivation not so much shared by his philosophical ancestors, a motivation to get answers to the existing philosophical questions. For all its precision and valuable insight about language, the approaches of the later analytic philosophers such as Wittgenstein and Austin had something defeatist about them, where the ability of philosophers to genuinely answer their questions was concerned.[5] Wittgenstein, for instance, argued that metaphysical claims could not coherently be made, and was fond of declaring the end of philosophy and urging his students not to become professional philosophers. Austin's approach also seemed to rule out the possibility of metaphysics, and in the eyes of critics reduced philosophy to something too close to linguistics. When Searle returned to the U.S. from Oxford in 1959 he brought with him not only expertise in the current school of linguistic philosophy, but also a renewed, more affirmative approach to philosophy in general.

The Defense of Realism

One of the highest forms of respect for a person, especially coming from a philosopher, is to argue with him. The willingness to engage in argument with someone signals respect for his ability to think clearly and to distinguish strong from weak arguments. Analytic philosophy in general is completely opposed to relativism - which can be described as the view that the truth of a statement is always relative to a person, place, or time - in all its forms. "Evolution may be true for *you*, but it's not true for *me*," is the sort of thing a relativist might claim. No doubt one reason why analytic philosophers tend not to be relativists is that the whole enterprise of philosophy rests on the idea that there is such a thing as getting it right. If relativism in a sweeping enough form is true, much of analytic philosophy rests on mistaken assumptions, mistaken enough to render the philosophy which rests on them moot. Disdain is the most frequently expressed attitude toward the practitioners of today's most popular form of relativism, known as deconstructionism, or more generally as what Searle calls *perspectivism*. If the relativists are genuinely mistaken though and not merely out of fashion, as Searle says, "we ought to be able to say exactly how and why."[6] In two recent books, *The Construction of Social Reality*, and *Mind, Language, and Society*, Searle has taken up the challenge of both refuting perspectivism and proving, in a limited way, realism - the view that there is a real world out there, with real objects possessing definite properties.

Searle offers a passage from a textbook on the philosophy of social science, which captures both the content and tone of perspectivism:

> Perspectivism is the view that all knowledge is essentially perspectival in character; that is, knowledge claims and their assessment always take place *within* a framework that provides the conceptual resources in and through which the world is described and explained. According to perspectivism, no one ever views reality directly as it is in itself; rather they approach it from their own slant with their own assumptions and preconceptions."[7]

Another claim typically made by perspectivists is that the different conceptual schemes are *incommensurable*, in that people employing one conceptual scheme cannot evaluate another conceptual scheme. There is no objective way to state or show that a conceptual scheme is correct, or that it is incorrect, according to this line of thought. In order for this to happen, there would have to be a super-perspective that encompassed all conceptual schemes, and allowed its users to pass judgement on them, exactly what perspectivists would deny is possible.

Searle considers and responds to several arguments for perspectivism:

An Argument From Conceptual Schemes

Humans rely on concepts in order to know and think about the world, on this all sides agree. Concepts must occur in a consistent system or at least in a system which seems consistent to the person who employs them. There are, however, an indefinitely large number of such systems, and while there may be certain pragmatic reasons for drawing the boundaries of a concept one way rather than another, the idea that conceptual boundaries correspond to real-world differences is a kind of myth, according to the perspectivist. Here is how Searle states the perspectivist's position:

External realism is false because we have no access to external reality except through our concepts. Different conceptual systems give different descriptions of reality, and these descriptions are inconsistent with each other.[8]

Searle's response is that the systems are not inconsistent. He takes up an example of Hilary Putnam's in which two different conceptual schemes give different answers to the question "How many objects are there in this room." One conceptual scheme which counts all of the furniture in the room gives the answer seven, while another scheme which counts a furniture set as one item gives the answer one. The answer to the question, how many things are there in the room, really, is both seven and one, depending on which system of measurement we are using, in the same way in which someone can weigh both 200 pounds and 91 kilograms. Harder cases, however, involve two different conceptual schemes which give contradictory results, for instance, to the question "Are this (red) and this (orange) the same color?" Do we say that the people who say yes to this question are simply wrong?

An Argument From Sense Data

All that we experience is a product of our brains, the perspectivist points out. Concentrate on your right hand. You seem to be sensing the hand itself, but amputees who experience phantom limbs have the same sensation, including feelings of hot or cold, and pains.[9] What you perceive is not the world, not your hand, but a set of carefully constructed representations which your brain is providing for you. Your brain receives input from your limbs, and structures the input into maplike representations which are (somehow) involved in producing your conscious experience of your body. Much the same story can be told about each of the other senses: What you experience in seeing, for instance, is the activity of certain retinotopic maps in your visual cortex, not objects "out there." Since you are not contacting the world itself but only your representations of it, it is wrong to say that you perceive the world.

Searle's response is that this argument is a version of the genetic fallacy: Attacking a belief because of the way the belief was arrived at, rather than actually giving evidence against the belief itself:

> The fact that I can give a causal account of how it comes about that I see the tree (light photons strike my retina and set up a series of neuron firings that eventually cause a visual experience) does not show that I don't see the tree.[10]

Yes, what we experience is a product of our brains, but these processes also allow us to experience the world itself.

One problem here is that the argument is muddied by a potentially serious confusion over the meaning of "see." This is another example of the systematic ambiguity between internal/first-person uses of words and external/third-person uses (see Chapter 2). One way to bring out the ambiguity is to describe a situation where the two different uses of "see" produce contrary results: When a person with red/green color blindness looks at a red square, does he see a red square, or does he see a green square? Which answer you give depends on which sense of "see" you employ. It sounds more correct to say that one *experiences* (or *apprehends*) conscious intentional states, saving "*see*" for cases in which there are external objects of perception: The color blind person is seeing red, but experiencing green. The perspectivist is focusing on the "internal" sense of "see," whereas Searle is focusing on the much more prevalent "external" sense. Note that in either case, however, a realist/materialist is going to claim that what you are in contact with (an inner, conscious state, or an external object) is part of the real, physical world. And, via that state, you are in contact with the world.

There is indeed an implicit dualism in the argument from sense data: Whatever we experience in the privacy of our own minds is not part of the real world. The dualism becomes especially absurd when descriptions of the causal processes of the brain are offered in support of this view. The brain is a physical thing like any other, and its causal interactions are causal interactions like any others.

An Argument From the Philosophy of Science

All theories in science are underdetermined by the data which they explain, in the sense that there are also an indefinitely large number of other theories which also explain that data. Both the Ptolemaic theory of the solar system, which places the earth at its center, and the Copernican theory, which places the sun at its center, can explain and predict the movements of all the planets, for example. Neither theory explains more of the data than the other or makes predictions not makeable by the other, so the theory we choose is simply a matter of our needs rather than a question of the way the world actually is, the perspectivist reasons. We prefer the Copernican theory because it is simpler. This makes it easier for us to employ it in making predictions about the movements of the planets, as well as in teaching it in the classroom.

According to Searle, however, the only way we are able to make sense out of the debate between the two theories is to assume that there really are planets out there, moving around in some way or other.[11] Simplicity is not an ultimate criterion for determining the truth of a theory. Rather it is only a useful heuristic for arriving at true theories. One sees the same sort of oversight when perspectivists argue that nothing is objective and that only the interests and opinions of people decide what counts as reality. What though is the perspectivist's ontology of these people? They seem to have rather definite properties; they definitely have certain opinions and interests.

Diagnosis

As always, Searle provides a diagnosis as to what exactly has misled his discussants. In the case of the perspectivist, it is that the perspectivist finds it

> repugnant that we, with our language, our consciousness, and our creative powers, should be subject to and answerable to a dumb, stupid, inert material world? Why shouldn't we think of the "real world" as something we create, and therefore something that is answerable to us? If all reality is a "social construction," then it is we who are responsible, not the world.[12]

This "will to power" and "desire for control" is coupled with a general "hatred of science" to reinforce the views of the perspectivist.[13] One suspects that perspectivism may be also a phase in the thinking of a society, in the same way that relativism is often a phase in an individual's ongoing development of a personal philosophy. Teachers of introductory courses in philosophy, English, anthropology and related disciplines can attest that undergraduates tend to espouse relativism when they espouse a philosophy. One useful thing philosophers can do is oppose such a trend, in the same way that they might point out alternatives to a society which has become dogmatic.

Another root of today's relativism, though, is the need for tolerance for differences in a diverse society. An argument like the following *seems* to connect this need for tolerance to relativism about truth:

The Tolerance Argument:

> We should respect the racial and cultural differences between people, and not insist that all people be alike.

Therefore, we should respect the different beliefs of others and not insist that there is only one correct set of beliefs.

To someone who accepts this argument, a realist philosopher who says such things as "some beliefs are true and the ones which are not true are false," sounds similar to someone who says "some races are acceptable and others are not." The problem with this argument is its failure to distinguish people's beliefs from their other properties, such as the way they look, or the music or art that they like, or the food they enjoy. While beliefs are either true or false according to the realist, colors, genders, music, and art are not. To insist that there are right or wrong skin colors, or only one right form of music or art, is to be racist at worst, and an intolerant boor at best.

In the realm of logic and reasoning, however, we are all the same in that the rules for good thinking make no mention of race, gender, or class. One of the most frequently-committed fallacies of good thinking is called *ad hominem* (Latin for "to the person"): Failure to separate the arguer's character or other features from *what* he said. Logic demands that in deciding the truth or reasonableness of a belief, we look only at the belief itself, ignoring everything about whoever holds it, in much the same way that moral and legal principles are color blind.[14] No race, gender or class has a monopoly on truth telling. Indeed, far from being intolerant, as I intimated above, engaging someone in dialogue and argument is a form of respect for her, for her ability to think and appreciate good and bad reasons for holding beliefs.

In *The Construction of Social Reality*, Searle provides an additional, more intellectual, diagnosis for the proliferation of perspectivism:

> One of the oldest urges in Western philosophy is to think that somehow or other truth and reality should coincide. That...if there really were such things as truth and reality...truth would have to provide an exact mirror of reality.... When the philosopher despairs of achieving an exact isomorphism between the structure of reality and the structure of true representations, the temptation is to think that somehow or other our naïve notions of truth and reality have been discredited.[15]

As long as the representation and the represented world are different things, there will be properties of the represented world not captured by the representation:

> There is a simple but deep reason why truth and reality cannot coincide in a way that many philosophers think.... The reason is this: All representation, and a fortiori all truthful representation, is always under certain aspects and not others. The aspectual character of all representation derives from such facts as that representation is always made from within a certain conceptual scheme and from a certain point of view.... In short, it is only from a point of view that we represent reality, but ontologically objective reality does not have a point of view.[16]

So representations only capture certain properties of the represented things, leaving out an indefinite number of other properties which the things possess. Incompleteness does not imply inaccuracy however. The ontologically objective thing out there has whatever properties it has; our different aspectual shapes single out certain of the thing's properties, but there are always properties the thing has which we either do not know about, or do not represent with our aspectual shapes.

Arguments For External Realism

Searle has argued that the opponents of external realism can be refuted, but can external realism be argued for directly? Searle admits that we cannot directly show that external realism is true, but he argues that we can show that when we attempt to communicate, we must assume external realism. The person who attempts to use language to claim that there is no external world is not necessarily contradicting himself, but given that we must assume external realism to understand what he is doing, his act becomes unintelligible.[17] This explains why there cannot be a non-question begging *argument* for external realism: The very fact that one is arguing requires a commitment to external realism.

We need to distinguish the truth conditions of a statement from what Searle calls the intelligibility conditions. The truth conditions for a statement are the conditions which must be met in order for that statement to be true. When we say that Clinton is left-handed, the primary truth conditions for this are that Clinton exists, and that he actually is left-handed. In order for us to understand that sentence in the normal way, we assume that it is about a real world; this is an intelligibility condition:

> A public language presupposes a public world in the sense that many (not all) utterances of a public language purport to make references to phenomena that are ontologically objective, and they ascribe such and such features to these phenomena. Now, in order that we should understand those utterances as having these truth conditions - the existence of these phenomena and the possession of these features - we have to take for granted that there is a way that the world is independent of our representations. But that requirement is precisely the requirement of external realism.[18]

Our ability to grasp the truth conditions of sentences rests on our more basic assumptions about the real world. We get at the nature of our commitment to the existence of an external world when we examine the way our background capacities (see Chapter 1) interact with the world outside. One way to get a grasp on the difference between truth conditions and intelligibility conditions is to see what happens when sentences deny either their own truth conditions, or their own intelligibility conditions. If you deny your utterance's truth conditions and say for instance: "The keys are in the car, and the keys are not in the car," you contradict yourself. When you deny one of your intelligibility conditions, and say "The keys are in the car, and external reality has never existed," you get a claim that is puzzling to us because it does not allow us our normal understanding of it.

Perspectivists frequently claim that real understanding is impossible, though, so they might simply reject the premise that communication really is successful: "Since you do not share my perspective, you cannot completely understand what I am saying. Perhaps it is futile for me to speak to you about my position, for that is what the position implies, as you say." Even this remark shows that the perspectivist is committed to his own existence, the fact that he is talking, the existence of his listener, and the fact that the listener understands at least some of his words. Even if these do not count as intelligibility conditions, they can involve the perspectivist in outright contradiction, evident in the following claims: "I am not talking (writing)," and "I do not exist."

Searle's Ontology

It is interesting to note that Searle needs to add the qualification that "ontologically *objective* reality does not have a point of view," in the quotation just above, since on his philosophy ontologically *subjective* reality involves only a single point of view. Someone who wanted to put the mental in the same ontological category as external physical objects might argue that another problem in trying to gain a true and complete representation of the world is that our mental representations are themselves physical things, so it is wrong to put them on one side, and the world on the other. Searle does not have this problem, but in making our mental representations - our intentional states - different from other things, he inherits other difficulties.

Many of the problems center around how ontologically objective and ontologically subjective properties interact. When unconscious aspectual shape (see Chapter 3) becomes conscious, for instance, what are the relations among the properties involved? How do the subjective properties come into being? Some ordinary properties have a curious way of appearing apparently out of nowhere, a phenomenon which has been called *emergence*. A single water molecule, for example, does not possess wetness, or liquidity, but when enough water molecules get together, the property of wetness emerges. Do subjective properties emerge in the same way that objective properties do? When they emerge, do they emerge from certain objective properties? One could put this another way by asking whether objective properties can cause subjective properties to come into being, in the way that the property of being black can cause a thing to become hot when exposed to the sun.

Truth as Correspondence

From the work of Tarski,[19] it is widely agreed among analytic philosophers that there is a basic template which any theory of truth should fit:

S is true if and only if p.

Where S is a sentence, and p is the condition under which that sentence is true. The linguistic feature of quotation can allow us to fill in the template for individual sentences, for instance:

"Snow is white" if and only if Snow is white.

Although this *disquotational* theory of truth looks trivial, Searle finds it useful because it embodies his claim that sentences are made

Reality

true by something outside of them.[20] This is just a particular example, however, Searle's general way to express his interpretation of the truth template is to say that:

> A statement is true if and only if it corresponds to the facts.

In order to interpret this correctly it is important the Searle's use of "fact" is understood in the right way. There are two quite different, competing definitions of the word "fact," only one of which Searle intends. When we say, "It is a fact that the Space Needle is in Seattle," what exactly are we calling a fact, that statement, "The Space Needle is in Seattle," or the actual Space Needle itself, actually located in Seattle itself? Is the fact the sentence (or something the sentence expresses), or the actual arrangement of objects in the world that makes the sentence true? According to Searle, the latter: Facts are concrete arrangements of objects in the world. Hence Searle is using "fact" the way that philosophers also use "state of affairs": a fact is literally something you can trip over.

"Correspondence" is the name of the relation between a true sentence and the fact that makes it true, on Searle's approach. There are a large number of ways in which statements can accurately represent facts, so "correspondence" cannot be given a brief, general definition.[21]

Searle's Legacy

How will Searle be seen as fitting into the history of 20th century philosophy? One suspects that he will be better remembered for his negative arguments, the Chinese room and the response to Quine, than for his positive theories about intentionality. These arguments may come to be seen as turning points in 20th Century thinking about the mind. It is also possible that Searle will be remembered for helping to make the discussion of consciousness again possible. Whether his solution to the mind-body problem or his theory of intentionality lasts depends on what direction these issues take as the different cognitive sciences continue their relentless uncovering of the brain's secrets.

One hears among professional philosophers a number of complaints about Searle, however, which threaten to lessen his influence, at least in their number. Searle's work is discussed in a wide variety of disciplines other than philosophy, though, which serves to counter any negative feelings among philosophers, and gives rise to lineages which may survive outside of the philosophical community. One frequently-heard complaint against Searle is that he is always begging the question, that is, simply assuming his position, then, not surprisingly, proving that his position is correct. One source of this is perhaps that Searle admittedly takes our conscious minds as a given, in the sense that our minds and what goes on in them is one of the main things to be explained, rather than something to be ignored or explained away. To someone who has decided that consciousness and the first-person point of view are irrelevant to say, how we understand language, Searle's use of them seems somehow unfair. The more interesting question, however, is whether the hypothesis of the conscious mind has led to good or bad results. If there is something deeply flawed in the notion of mind or consciousness, or the idea that we have mental states which represent the world, this should be all the more apparent when Searle tries to extend those notions and regiment them into theory.

A second accusation made against Searle is that he plays on his reader's intuitions. In the original replies published with the Chinese room argument, there were ominous accusations by several of the respondents that Searle had somehow tricked his readers by playing on their intuitions. Ned Block said that the "appeal to intuition" was a "point against Searle"[22] and that the intuitions in question might reveal only "prejudices, ignorance" or a "lack of imagination--as when people accepted the deliverance of intuition that two straight lines cannot cross twice." Dennett accused Searle of "relying on ill-gotten gains; favorable intuitions generated by misleadingly presented thought experiments," as well as using what he called an "intuition pump." Such a pump is not, said Dennett, "an engine of discovery, but a persuader or pedagogical tool--a way of getting people to see things your way once you've seen the truth, as Searle thinks he has."[23]

Implied in this of course is the idea that these intuitions are not to be trusted. We know that *certain* intuitions are notoriously mistaken, such as the intuition that a stick in water is bent, when actually it is straight, or the intuition to think of the earth as flat. But, the fact that some intuitions are mistaken does not imply that they all are, or even that they all might be. What exactly is the *general* reason why intuitions should not be trusted?

A third criticism, that Searle hides hideous complexity under simple slogans and catch-phrases, depends for its force on the source of the complexity. If the complexity is due to peculiarities of the writer, that is a bad kind of complexity, but if it is due to the phenomena themselves, that is a kind of complexity which is necessary. It is necessary for the same reason that a scientific theory which is fruitful, in that it leads to new ideas and experiments, is better than one which is seemingly unassailable, but barren. The possibility needs to be left open that Searle in fact has used a few simple phrases to project us into the maws of the problem under discussion, and that the complexity we are seeing is the complexity of mind or language themselves.

One source of misunderstanding may be the simplicity and clarity of Searle's writing. Simple writing tends to make the person who believes that difficult problems can only be solved with difficult language suspicious. Often the accusation is made that Searle sweeps massively complex problems under the rug of simple observations. These criticisms may partly reflect the state of academic philosophy, or perhaps more broadly, a difference in basic philosophical temperaments between Searle and his philosophical readers. This is a difference between philosophers who are genuinely interested in solving problems and those who are merely engaging in a certain kind of dialogue. The latter type may also believe that the problems are not solvable. Surely everyone will agree that Searle is clear as to what problem he is solving and how he intends to solve it. One thing in abundance in a Searle book is arguments for proposed solutions to problems. In most philosophical circles, including analytic philosophy, it is considered naïve, or at best presumptuous to actually offer solutions, especially to major problems. One is supposed to undertake a fine-grained analysis of a part of a problem or certain of its proposed solutions. It is important that the written report of this analysis be rather difficult to read, this is a mark of expertise in a field, on the assumption that if you do not speak in a jargon, you are not a professional of any sort. The philosopher who wishes to engage in logical repartee is disappointed when he fails to find in Searle's writing the sort of dense tangle of arguments and intricate distinctions which tickles his mental fancy in just the right way.

This sort of attitude is partly due to the idea that each academic discipline is a highly specialized field that people in other fields and especially non-academics should not expect to understand. Against this trend, one of Searle's best characteristics is his accessibility both to philosophers and to everyone else, and his insistence that the hardest philosophical positions and debates can be explained simply.

Endnotes

[1] G.J. Warnock, *English Philosophy Since 1900*, Oxford: Oxford Univ. Press, 1969.

[2] *Ibid.*, p. 13.

[3] *Ibid.*, pp. 15-16.

[4] *The Philosophy of G.E. Moore*, ed. P.A. Schilpp, Evanston Ill., 1942, p. 14.

[5] See Searle's response to Norman Malcolm's article "I Believe that p" in *John Searle and His Critics*, eds. Ernest Lepore and Robert Van Gulick, Oxford: Basil Blackwell, 1991, for Searle's criticisms of the limits of the techniques of ordinary language philosophy, pp. 185-188.

[6] "Indeterminism, Empiricism, and the First Person," *The Journal of Philosophy*, **LXXXIV** (1987), p. 123.

[7] Brian Fay, *Contemporary Philosophy of Social Science*, Oxford: Blackwell, 1996, p. 72.

[8] *Mind, Language, and Society*, pp. 22-23.

[9] See "The Perception of Phantom Limbs," V.S. Ramachandran and William Hirstein, *Brain*, **121** (1998), pp. 1603-1630.

[10] *Mind, Language, and Society*, p. 29.

[11] *Ibid.*, p. 25.

[12] *Ibid.*, p. 32.

[13] *Mind, Language, and Society*, p. 33.

[14] Melinda Campbell pointed out to me both the connection between relativism and the need for tolerance, as well as the idea that we are viewed as the same for legal and moral purposes.

[15] *The Construction of Social Reality*, p. 175.

[16] *Ibid.*, pp. 175-176.

[17] *Ibid.*, p. 189.

[18] *Ibid.*, pp. 186-187.

[19] See Tarski's article, "The Concept of Truth in Formalized Languages," in Logic, Semantics, Metamathematics, Oxford: Clarendon Press, 1956.

[20] *The Construction of Social Reality*, p. 202.

[21] As, for example, Wittgenstein attempts to do with his picture theory of language. See A.J. Ayer's book, *Wittgenstein*, New York: Random House, 1985, for a description of the picture theory.

[22] Ned Block, "What Intuitions About Homunculi Don't Show," *The Behavioral and Brain Sciences*, **3** (1980), pp. 425-426.

[23] See Dennett's original response to the Chinese room argument, "The Milk of Human Intentionality," *The Behavioral and Brain Sciences*, **3**, pp. 428-430.

Biographical Note

John Rogers Searle was born in Denver, Colorado in 1932. His father was an electrical engineer, his mother a medical doctor. He attended the University of Wisconsin, Madison from 1949 to 1952, focusing on the natural and social sciences as well as the humanities. At the age of 19, in his junior year, Searle was awarded a Rhodes scholarship to study at Oxford. There he pursued a degree in philosophy, politics and economics, and was tutored in philosophy by James Urmson and Peter Strawson, two of the most prominent analytic philosophers in the post-Wittgensteinian period of the 40s and 50s. Oxford at this point was the philosophical capital of the world. Among its professors were some of the most well-known active philosophers, including J.L. Austin and Gilbert Ryle. Philosophical discussion went on constantly, inside class as well as out, either in the undergraduate philosophy societies or informally after classes. Searle was tutored by Strawson in his third year at Oxford, and Strawson ultimately had a huge influence in setting Searle's basic philosophical outlook.

When his scholarship was up, Searle was prepared to return to the U.S. to seek an advanced degree but at the last minute received a second scholarship which allowed him to stay at Oxford. He remained there for three more years, working as a lecturer and tutor and studying with Strawson, Austin, and Peter Geach. As a lecturer, Searle was considered a full-fledged member of the faculty during this time. Searle says,

> In those days you could be a faculty member just on the strength of your BA. I did a D.Phil degree while I was a faculty member at Christ Church, and I only did the D.Phil because I wanted to come back to the United States. If you got a good BA (a first [in the examinations]) that was all you needed in Oxford.[1]

Geach was the director of Searle's dissertation, submitted in 1959, on the subject of sense and reference.

Searle had married in 1958, to Dagmar Carboch, who was also a philosophy student, and in the fall of 1959 they moved to California. There Searle began his teaching career at the University of California, Berkeley, where he has remained ever since. After a year as a visiting professor at the University of Michigan in Ann Arbor, Searle returned to Berkeley for the 1962-63 academic year. The next year, he spent his sabbatical at M.I.T. studying generative grammars with Noam Chomsky. He then returned to Oxford for the Spring term of 1964, where he completed a draft of what would become his first book,

Speech Acts.

The Berkeley to which Searle returned in the Fall of 1964 had changed greatly. The student unrest that became the free speech movement was soon in full swing, and Searle was heavily involved in the conflict between students and University administrators. He spoke frequently in defense of the students' right to free speech, and was eventually appointed Special Assistant for Student Affairs, a position he occupied during the height of the unrest, from 1965 to 1967. His involvement was so great during this period that he was unable to complete *Speech Acts* until he took a leave of absence for the 1967-68 academic year to return to Oxford where he completed the book. In 1970 Searle was invited to the White House to work as a faculty representative to the Heard Commission on student unrest, and in 1971 he published an account of the free speech movement called *The Campus War*, and

With the end of the student upheavals in the early 1970s, Searle returned to philosophy full-time and in 1983 published his primary work in the philosophy of mind, *Intentionality*. In the late 1970s, he became more active in the developing field of cognitive science, and in 1980 published the enormously influential article in which he laid out the "Chinese room" argument against the idea that the mind is a computer program. This article gave rise to an intense debate between Searle and the defenders of the new computational view of the mind, and resulted in Searle's being asked in 1984 to deliver the Reith lectures on the BBC in England. These lectures were published as Searle's first book for non-philosophers, *Minds, Brains and Science*.

During the period from the mid-eighties up to the publication of *The Rediscovery of the Mind* in 1992, Searle expanded his theory of intentionality by explaining the relevance of consciousness to the human brain's ability to achieve representation. The mid-nineties marked a resurgence in Searle's interest in the social dimensions of language use, and in intentional states which are shared by two or more people. The results of this work are described in his 1995 *book The Construction of Social Reality*. In this book Searle also explored various anti-relativist arguments, an interest he is continuing to follow in a book he is currently writing on the subject of rationality.

---

[1] Personal email communication.

Bibliography

Selected Works

1958: "Russell's Objections to Frege's Theory of Sense and Reference," *Analysis*, **18**, pp. 137-143.

"Proper Names," *Mind*, **67**, pp. 166-173.

1964: "How to Derive 'Ought' From 'Is'," *The Philosophical Review*, **73**, pp. 43-58.

1965: "What is a Speech Act?" in *Philosophy in America*, ed. Max Black, London: Allen and Unwin, pp. 221-239.

1969: *Speech Acts: An Essay in the Philosophy of Language*, Cambridge: Cambridge University Press.

1979: *Expression and Meaning: Studies in the Theory of Speech Acts*, Cambridge: Cambridge University Press.

1980: "Minds, Brains, and Programs," *The Behavioral and Brain Sciences*, **3**, pp. 417-457.

1981: "Analytic Philosophy and Mental Phenomena," in *The Foundations of Analytic Philosophy: Midwest Studies in Philosophy, Volume VI*, eds. Peter A. French, Theodore E. Uehling, Jr., and Howard K. Wettstein, Minneapolis: University of Minnesota Press, pp. 405-423.

1982: "The Chinese Room Revisited," *The Behavioral and Brain Sciences*, **5**, pp. 345-348.

1983: *Intentionality: An Essay in the Philosophy of Mind*, Cambridge: Cambridge University Press.

1984: *Minds, Brains and Science*, Harvard University Press.

"Intentionality and its Place in Nature," *Synthese*, **61**, pp. 3-16.

1987: "Intentionality, Empiricism, and the First Person," *Journal of*

Philosophy, **84**, pp. 123-146.

1989: "Consciousness, Unconsciousness, and Intentionality," *Philosophical Topics*, **XVII**, pp. 193-209.

1990: "Is the Brain's Mind a Computer Program?," *Scientific American*, Jan., pp. 26-31.

1992: *The Rediscovery of the Mind*, Cambridge, Mass.: The M.I.T. Press.

"Rationality and Realism: What is at Stake," *Daedelus,* **122**, pp. 55-84.

1995: *The Construction of Social Reality*, New York: The Free Press.

1996: "Contemporary Philosophy in the United States," in *The Blackwell Companion to Philosophy*, eds. Nicholas Bunnin and E.P. Tsui-James, Oxford: Blackwell Publishers Ltd.

1997: *The Mystery of Consciousness*, New York: The New York Review of Books.

1998: *Mind, Language and Society: Philosophy in the Real World*, New York: Basic Books.